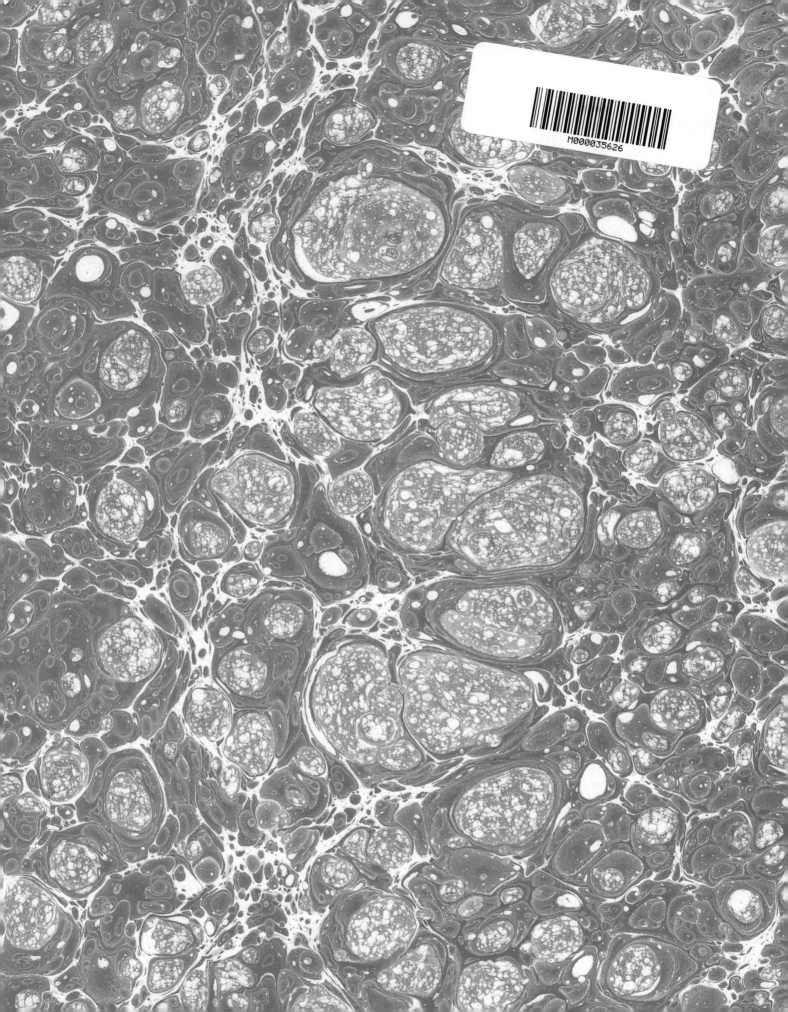

NORITAKE
COLLECTIBLES A TO Z

A PICTORIAL
RECORD
& GUIDE
TO VALUES

880 Lower Valley Road, Atglen, PA 19310 USA

DAVID SPAIN

I dedicate this book to my wife, Jannie Chow Spain and to our daughter, Rachel Lin Spain with love, admiration and gratitude.

Library of Congress Cataloging-in-Publication Data

Spain, David H.
    Noritake collectibles, A to Z: a pictorial record & guide to values / David H. Spain.
            p.   cm.
    Includes bibliographical references and index.
    ISBN: 0-7643-0057-1
    1. Noritake, Kabushiki Kaisha--Collectibles--Catalogs.
    2. Porcelain, Japanese--20th century--Catalogs.
  I. Title.
    NK4210.N56A4   1997
    738.2'0952'1674--dc21
                                    97-11385
                                    CIP

ISBN: 0-7643-0057-1

Printed in China

Published by Schiffer Publishing, Ltd.
4880 Lower Valley Road
Atglen, PA 19310
Phone: (610) 593-1777
Fax: (610) 593-2002
E-mail:Schifferbk@aol.com
Please write for a free catalog.
This book may be purchased from the publisher.
Please include $2.95 for shipping.
Try your bookstore first.

We are interested in hearing from authors
with book ideas on related subjects.

Designed by Bonnie M. Hensley

Contents

Acknowledgments

This, I must confess, is not my first book. In each of those other projects, I happily began, as I do here, by acknowledging the many debts acquired during the project's creation. This point in the book-writing process always startles me because I am so forcefully reminded that it takes so many people to produce something as seemingly simple as a book.

As great as my debts may have been in other projects, they pale in comparison to those I have accumulated in the process of creating this book. If I were merely to list all those who have aided me in this book's completion, you might well think you were holding a phone book. If I were to describe, even briefly, all the substantial kindnesses shown to me in the course of my efforts, a great portion of the pages in this book would be filled with those remarks. In the 18 months I spent working on this book, I have often referred to it as a "labor of love." Although true, this common enough sentiment is easily misunderstood. This book is not simply a product of *my* love for the subject; it is rather the result of the love of many people, not only for the subject but more importantly, for each other. To experience this phenomenon firsthand has, and continues to be, genuinely awe inspiring for me.

Everyone I called upon for help did what they could when they were asked. Of some people, I asked a great deal and I want to begin by thanking them, not only sincerely but also, in keeping with the structure of this book, in alphabetical order. Happily, this method permits me to begin with Margaret Louise Anderson who, through her tremendous efforts and the help of her mother Marian, has provided you with the opportunity to see some of her marvelous photographs. As you look through this book, gasping and thinking to yourself, "what a wonderful photograph," it is a good bet that photo is one of Margaret's.

I am equally pleased to acknowledge a wonderful decade of boundless hospitality and assistance, in separate and distinct ways, from my good friends Marilyn and Norm Derrin. As you look at this book and notice an elegant, amazing piece that is unlike anything you have ever seen before, the chances are good that it is one of Norm's or Marilyn's. Unless, that is, the piece belongs to either Mark Griffin or Earl Smith who, as it happens, were among the first to be subjected to my invasion with camera, tripod, and all the disruption that comes with them. Earl, in particular, has been most cordial and helpful to me for the nearly 10 years I have known him—even though we have at times held differing views on matters of substance to Noritake collectors. Therefore, I am especially grateful for his support of this project. For many of the same reasons, I wish to thank and honor three of my friends who have authored books like this one: Lou Ann Donahue, Joan Van Patten, and Carole Bess White. Their books on Noritake and Japanese collectibles have inspired and aided me in countless ways during this project. Without their books by my side every step of the way, I simply could not have completed this work.

There are many photographs in this book that, although certainly adequate, may not strike you as exceptional. It would be a serious error, however, to think of those photographs as "ordinary." We all should remember that one cannot tell, simply by looking at a photograph, how much effort and love has gone into producing it. I have had the privilege of learning this lesson primarily through the experiences of many collector friends who made valiant efforts to produce photographs for this book. In this sense, some amazing (and truly fine) photographs in this book were provided by the loving labor of Donna and Doug Bingaman, Dr. Dennis and Susan Buonafede, Sherry Brooks, Judi Camero, Michael Conrad, Jean Dillard (with the help of her husband Joe and her family), Dana Dwaileebe, Bebe and Fred Geisler, Mary Lou Gross, Truman P. Hawes, Greg Heiden, Brian and Yvonne Hurst, Gary Kaufman (who provided scores of photos from his wonderful collection), Janet Keller, Pat and Mike Kocor, Diane Kovarik, Vicki Lee Little, Tom and Cille Mathis, Bill and Christopher Phillipson, Bob Suslowicz, and Lori and Dennis Trishman. For their assistance with other aspects of this project, I thank the following collectors (and friends): Beverly Anderson, Nancee Blaney, Elizabeth Cohee, Deirdre Cimiano, Lisa Gibson, Joe and Deanna Liotta, Rhonda, John and Daryl Perroncino, Tim and Janet Trapani, Ed and Joan Vanzo, Joe and Rhoda Westler, and Barbara and Jim Winfree.

Given that long list of names, I suppose I should note that I actually shot some of the photographs that appear in this book. That I was able to do so was, in no small measure, because many friends in all parts of North America welcomed me into their homes to handle the most precious pieces in their collections and disrupt their lives for hours or sometimes days. In this regard, I am delighted to thank those who not only put up with me, but also who put me up in their homes during my journeys to their part of this continent. In addition to Marilyn Derrin, Mark Griffin, and Earl Smith, I am touched by the hospitality shown to me by Joane McCaslin Freguson and her husband Bruce, Bob and Linda Trennert, and my son Andrew Spain. On such journeys, I was privileged to photograph portions of my hosts' collections as well as those of Claire and Michael Conrad, Patricia Engel, Bob and Bernadette Jackson, Laurie Larson, Ken and Janet Lodge, Jim Martin (who also went to the trouble of packing up much of his collection and hauling it to and from the photography location), Bob Suslowicz, and Fred Tenney. I am grateful to all of these people for their generosity and interest in this project.

I also managed to shoot quite a few photographs closer to home. For reasons yet unknown, there appears to be an especially strong interest in Noritake collecting in the Pacific Northwest. I have been encouraged and inspired in many ways by these fellow collectors and neighbors. In this regard, I thank Dick and Alice Bartelt, Gary Goodman and Joanna Beckley Goodman, Kimberly Carman, Dick and Sally Nelson, and Nancy and Charlie Wilson. Those who know the Northwest collectors will have noticed that, alphabetically speaking at least, I have skipped some rather important names. This I did intentionally, because I wish to focus particular attention on four people whose contributions to this endeavor have been *enormous*.

I refer to Sheldon and Sayo Harmeling and Mike and Connie Owen. Sheldon and Sayo are known to many, far and wide, as extraordinary Noritake collectors. I and others fortunate enough to think of these two as good friends, know them to be extraordinary people. It would take a page simply to list all the ways Sheldon and Sayo have helped me with this book and other matters over the past 9 years. The same may be said for Connie and Mike. Of all those mentioned here, I have known and loved Mike and Connie the longest—nearly 30 years. In 1989, *the* newsletter for collectors of and dealers in Noritake collectibles,

Noritake News, was launched with Mike's vital encouragement and expert printing skills. I have been aided by Mike in many other ways–in particular by his willingness, on countless occasions and seemingly limitless hours, to *listen* . . . and I must add, by his very dry wit. Connie, as is her wont and special knack, has been the nurturer for so many others and for me, especially when I have needed it most.

A wise pediatrician once said (puzzlingly at first), "There is no such thing as a baby." What he (and it was a "he"–D.W. Winnicott, by name) meant is that one cannot hope to understand babies without also understanding their parents. Put another way, he was saying that because babies are unable to survive without parents (mothers in particular), it is vital to think about babies and parents *together*. By the same token, one may say, "There is no such thing as a collector." To understand collectors, you must also understand dealers. Over the years, I have come to know many antiques dealers and some deserve special acknowledgment here–not for being dealers *per se,* but for helping me improve this book in many ways. In this regard, I am happy to thank G. Lynd Bingham, Bill and Judy Boyd, Jeff Figmaka, Doris and George Myers, Beverly Rosenow, and Gerri and Tom Seitz. As previously, I have skipped a few names to give special emphasis to those dealers who have not only become my good friends but also have made significant contributions to this book–namely, Dennis Burnickas and Diane Vilkanskas, Carrie and Gerry Domitz (it was they who found and sold to me the double-backstamped piece discussed elsewhere in this book), Brian and Yvonne Hurst, Patricia Leon, and Chloe McKinney.

Until very recently, few in Japan were aware that the Noritake Company had produced the wonderful porcelains shown in this book. This is changing, thanks in part to donations to the Noritake Museum by Lou Ann Donahue and the late Howard Kottler, among others. This museum is visited annually by hundreds of people, most of them Japanese. There is now an active and growing market for Noritake collectibles in Japan and a few collectors are members of the Noritake Col-America. Of these collectors, I wish to thank Tomoko Nakashima for helping me with certain details about Noritake backstamps and for other kindnesses.

I also am honored to thank Mr. Keishi Suzuki for providing me with various historical photographs of the Noritake Company, its founders, some of its products, and the complete line of Noritake Christmas Bells, Valentine Hearts, and Easter Eggs. In addition, his words of encouragement are of great significance to me. I am impressed as well by the support and encouragement I received from the Noritake Company's Bill Donahue. All those associated with this great company should be as energetic and enthusiastic as he is.

I conclude finally with a few words about my friends and family. It is they who on the most regular basis have put up with me not only in general, but also specifically with what can only be described as my Noritake mania. Hanging around collectors, when you yourself are not a collector, must be a lot like listening to deer hunters when you don't hunt deer. It can be fascinating for a few minutes, but soon enough, the stories become repetitive and irrelevant (to put it nicely). So, for not letting on that I was as boring as I must have been, I want to thank Mike, Peggy, and Alex Evans, Faith Fogarty, Margot Kenly and Bill Cumming, Stu, Sue, and Jordana Heller, Roy and Judy Lawton, Chris, Jyl and Alex Leininger, Tom and Margaret Lopez, Scott Malatos and Louisa Gowen, Heather and Greg Oaksen, Simon and Carol Ottenberg, Mary and Pat Ragen, Barbara and Jim Sand, and last but not least, Robert Schneider, whose collecting instincts have long inspired me.

As for my family: everyone knows that words are not adequate to the task. *Family* means the sort of feelings that are captured in unsung words only by gifted poets. My adult sons, Andrew and Ryan, have and continue to be a tremendous source of pride and comfort for me. Without the assistance, tolerance, and love of my wife and daughter, however, this book quite simply would not be.

David H. Spain
Seattle, Spring 1997

PART ONE
Chapter 1

Introduction: The Aim and Scope of This Book

Purpose and Organization of the Book

My primary goal, in preparing this book, was to photographically present a large and representative sample of the thousands of non-dinnerware porcelains produced by the Noritake Company between approximately 1908 and the present. Although I will say more about the matter, it may be noted that the scope of this book is greater than any previous book on what are known as "Noritake" collectibles, especially when these pieces are being referred to by North American collectors and dealers (later in this chapter, I indicate why there must be quotation marks around the word "Noritake" here). The extent to which this goal has been achieved may be judged somewhat by examining Part Two of this book.

My second, yet still basic, goal is to present this material—photographs and captions alike—so that both dealers and collectors can *quickly and easily* make good use of it. This task was, by far, the most challenging part of producing this book. As authors before me have already learned, I found that creating a simple, easy-to-use reference work adds considerably to the demanding task of book production. For this reason, I offer my thoughts about the rationale for this book's organization.

In Part One of this book, I discuss historical and technical issues. In Chapter 2, I briefly review the history of the Noritake Company and discuss trends and developments in the field of Noritake collecting. In Chapter 3, I examine as briefly as possible the arcane and technical issue of Noritake backstamps. The 11 chapters in Part Two contain nearly all of the 1200-plus photographs in this book. I am certain this is the part of the book that readers will make the most use of. Accordingly, I gave considerable thought to how the material in those chapters should be organized.

Ultimately, Part Two was structured in light of one simple fact: most people, even those well-versed in this field, generally consult this type of book when they want information about a specific piece that they own or one that they are thinking of buying or selling. In other words, the readers' goals tend to be specific rather than general, although there will be users of this book who have general goals about the field of Noritake collecting and dealing. Many readers who consult this book will have such goals, and I believe their needs can also be met with the materials arranged and documented herein. My principal objective has been to arrange the material so that a variety of readers (vis a vis the field of Noritake collecting) may all quickly and thoroughly satisfy their needs.

At first, I worried that creating a book for readers to use much like a dictionary or encyclopedia would all but exclude the needs of advanced collectors or dealers who wanted general information about the field. Eventually, it occurred to me that the needs of these two audience groups were not incompatible. Indeed, I thought, properly done, a book created to satisfy the basic needs of the infrequent user could at the same time meet the needs of collectors or dealers already familiar with this field. The result was my decision to organize Part Two into alphabetical chapters.

To understand the layout and intended use of Part Two, the reader need only recall the layout and use of a multivolume encyclopedia, with alphabetically arranged entries. An encyclopedia user is not likely to sit down and read the text from cover to cover. Rather, the reader would turn to an encyclopedia for a specifically listed topic. In most cases, readers will want quick information on a subject and will look for alphabetically arranged entries related to the information they need. Much like the multivolume encyclopedia, the chapters in Part Two are sequenced alphabetically. The topics *within* the chapters are also arranged alphabetically.

An alternative layout, of course, would have been to arrange the materials another way and direct the user to a comprehensive index. This approach was not adopted here, however, because a detailed index would be quite frustrating for the reader if he or she simply wanted to locate a "vase" or "bowl," since hundreds of such pieces are shown in this book. Of course, an author could try differentiating bowls in the index by sizes, shapes, or motifs. Indeed, an index could be constructed that would be quite detailed, containing many systems of features and characteristics likely to be of interest to collectors and dealers with a wide variety of special interests.

However admirable this endeavor might be, an index such as this presumes three things that I do not: 1) the typical user of such a book would enjoy wading through a detailed index; 2) the user and author would generally agree on what information must be known to use such an index; and 3) the typical reader would consult an index before looking at the photographs in an effort to find a particular piece. From experience and from speaking with both dealers and collectors, I know that most of us look at the photos first. Then, if we have not found the information we are looking for, we turn to the index for help. Early on, I decided to accept this fact rather than fight it.

Don't get me wrong. There is an index in this book, and I believe you will find it useful. There is, however, an easier, more enjoyable way to find a piece in this book than by consulting the index. With this method, the reader must do just three simple things: 1) note what *general type* of piece it is; 2) use the *table of contents* to find the chapter which discusses that type of piece; and 3) read the first paragraph of that chapter, which lists the page numbers where specific kinds of the type are located.

You, the reader, can make this process even simpler. This is because, as you may have noticed from the Contents, the chapters in Part Two are designated by a *letter* followed by the chapter title. These letters were selected to serve as a *mnemonic*, or an aid to memory. The chapter letters will enable you to skip the table of contents. For example, Chapter B contains information about bowls and boxes. Once you know this, whenever you want information about a bowl or box, you can simply turn to Chapter B. Because the chapters in Part Two are sequenced alphabetically and the chapter titles are on the righthand pages, it is fairly easy to find the chapter you need simply by flipping the pages.

The rationale for grouping the pieces in a single chapter requires virtually no explanation, and the mnemonic of the chapter designation is usually obvious. This is, I admit, less clear for some chapters. Consider Chapter T, for example. It is so designated because it is the place in this book where photos of tea sets can be found. As a quick glance at that chapter will show, however, one will encounter photos of many other kinds of things before coming to the tea sets.

To fully understand the rationale for the content of that and other simlarly organized chapters, the reader must note the chapter title. These titles were created to provide the reader quickly with two vital bits of information: 1) the total content of the chapter; and 2) why these contents are grouped together. For example, in Chapter T, the key words of the title in this respect are "Other Items Related to Beverages." Thus, Chapter T (unlike B) is not simply about one or two types of Noritake (where "types" are based on the basic functions of a piece).

So far, this method may seem simple and obvious enough; it may even be obvious why the reader will find cream and sugar sets in Chapter T. All of this information can seem quite puzzling, however, if the reader has noticed that there is a chapter on "Condiment Sets and Related Items." If a "condiment" is defined as something that one can eat *with* food but not *as* food, then by this definition, it would seem that cream and sugar sets should be in Chapter C, not Chapter T. If "problems" such as this occur frequently, there may be doubt as to whether I have succeeded in organizing the contents in a manner that will meet the specific needs of the infrequent reader.

Whether or not it appears as such in all cases, there are reasons for the placement of these pieces. More importantly, I predict that most of these reasons will seem adequate even if they fall short of one or another ideal. These reasons are discussed briefly at the beginning of each chapter, so I needn't discuss them in any detail here. Rather, I simply acknowledge up front that I cannot totally defend the content decisions made for every item of every chapter. This is because some of the pieces shown could be placed, with good reason, in several chapters. My decisions about the location of pieces were not based simply on my own ideas; they were the result of consultations with many people, especially in difficult cases. Consequently, I am fairly confident that you will quickly see the rationale and be able to use this format to simplify your use of this book. Certainly, this has always been my goal.

One final comment about the organization of this book is necessary. Many collectors (and I among them) tend to think in terms of motifs (decorative form) rather than blanks (function) and moreover, are far more interested in some motifs than others. Not only that, collectors love to see diverse items with the same or similar motifs grouped together. Therefore, it was extremely tempting to organize the book around motifs rather than blanks, as has been done. Indeed, one of the early outlines for this book was based on an "organize-by-motif" premise. Had this plan been adopted, there could have been chapters on Art Deco Florals, Geometrics, or Traditional Scenics, among many others.

That is just the point: there are so *many* motifs. Moreover, although there are some motifs that virtually anybody can recognize ("geometrics" is one of the more clear-cut examples), most are far less obvious. For example, what are the features which mark a floral motif as "Art Deco" in character? One solution to this problem, of course, would be to place a piece with *any* floral motif in a bigger chapter called Chapter F: Florals. As I mentioned, it was very tempting to do this.

Ultimately, I did not adopt the motif method. First, I felt that more problems would arise because of Noritake pieces which combined the usual motif categories of interest, than because of pieces that could be placed in several chapters based on function. Second, although many collectors think in terms of mo-

tifs, this is by no means an overwhelming trend. Third, most dealers and those who are neither Noritake collectors nor dealers (i.e., that large group of users who will consult this book for very specific needs), will tend to think more often in terms of function than in motif (i.e., in terms of "candlestick," rather than "yellow floral"). In short, the book was organized with the needs of the majority in mind. I earnestly hope the results will work well for you.

The Scope of This Book, or What is a "Noritake Collector?"

Toward the beginning of this chapter, I noted that quotation marks were needed around the word "Noritake." I now present my promised explanation. To refresh your memory, I said: "the scope of this book is far greater than any previous book on what are known as 'Noritake' collectibles, especially when being referred to by North American collectors and dealers."

I put quotation marks around the word "Noritake" to indicate that it is a word whose meaning varies so greatly that no one can easily assume to know what it means. In fact, the more I think about it, the more difficult it becomes to provide a definition that would enable someone to know precisely what the term "Noritake collector" means *in practice*. It may be best to say that the term means whatever any person demonstrates that it means by his or her actions as a "Noritake collector."

Frequently, that is what I say when people ask me to define the term. Just as often, however, people find this answer completely unhelpful (if not downright annoying). Moreover, such an answer provides no help at all for persons who wish to know whether their views of themselves as "Noritake collectors" at all correspond to those which had a bearing on the scope of this book. Therefore, I will attempt to clarify matters a bit. The reader is forewarned: the discussion that follows is somewhat nit-picky, and after all of it, many issues will be left either undiscussed or unresolved. In short, although this appears a simple issue to address, it is in fact a surprisingly complicated subject.

Although much of the discussion here will focus on the word "Noritake," a very important part of the sentence from the outset of this chapter and quoted above is the phrase "North American collectors." This is not because the "Noritake collectors" from this part of the world are more important than others; rather, it is because these collectors uphold what other collectors from England and Japan believe to be rather odd views on a matter of importance to this book. This matter concerns the very definition of a "Noritake collectible."

To the uninitiated, this should seem an easy matter to resolve. Wouldn't it make sense to say that "Noritake collectors" are people who collect "Noritake collectibles," and that "Noritake collectibles" are porcelains made by the Noritake Company? Yes, this explanation would make sense, and as it happens, this definition would not be entirely wrong. It would not be entirely right either, and therein lies the conceptual tale we must consider.

Before getting into the details, I note that for the most part, the problem is not one of "debate" about the right answer. Each experienced collector from North America seems to know quite well what he or she means by the term "Noritake collector." Also for the most part, it appears that nearly any two of them will agree regarding what they and others mean by the term. Even so, most of them would be hard-pressed to provide a *simple and adequate* formal definition of the term. I know that I myself have not found it easy to do.

As a general phenomenon, by the way, this is not particularly unusual. Words take on meanings through use, and use implies some type of context. By contrast, formal definitions tend to be thought of, better or worse, as a function of how context-free they appear to be. This concept helps us to understand how we correctly use words we can't define or words which, if defined, would provoke legitimate dissent from others. This point also explains how biologists can initiate extended and serious debates about the formal definition of a word as important and often-used by them as, say, "species." Philosophers too, it sometimes seems, do little else than debate about the meanings of words. Although the case of "Noritake collectors" is similar to these examples in some respects, the circumstances are different and important enough to warrant discussion.

Let me begin by presenting an example. Imagine that you have been invited to the home of an avid, knowledgeable, and very experienced porcelain collector living in North America. Imagine further that both you and the collector know that the majority of the elegant pieces in his or her home were made by the Noritake Company for export to the United States. Could you be sure, knowing this, that this person is a "Noritake collector?" If you answered "no," move to the head of the class. All of these facts could be true for this collector, but he or she might think of him- or herself as anything but a "Noritake collector."

Why? Well, in the simplest terms, this is due to an "historical accident." Prior to 1921, because of U.S. laws regarding the labeling of goods imported to the United States, most of the Noritake porcelains exported to the *United States* (and this point is vital) had backstamps which included neither the words "Noritake" nor "Japan." Instead, most often only the words "handpainted" and the Anglicized version of the Japanese word for "Japan" were found; that word is "Nippon." Thus, given the facts of the case, the not-entirely fictitious collector described above would, almost certainly, refer to him- or herself as a "Nippon collector."

To better understand not only the hypothetical collector just described but also a "Noritake collector," it will help to consider this case a bit more. Can one conclude that "Nippon collectors" are people who collect porcelains made and exported to the United States only by the Noritake Company prior to 1921? Again, if you answered "no," take a bow. As it happens, many self-described "Nippon collectors" are interested in any porcelain marked "Nippon" (assuming, of course, that the form or function of the piece appeals to their collecting preferences), whether or not the Noritake Company produced it.

To review, we have reached two conclusions so far. First, not all people who collect porcelains made by the Noritake Company are "Noritake collectors;" some are known as "Nippon collectors." Second, not all those who collect "Nippon" are interested exclusively in porcelains made by the Noritake Company.

What about "Noritake collectors?" Can we conclude, from the above, that most "Noritake collectors" may be defined as people who collect porcelains made for export by the Noritake Company whether or not they are marked with the words "Noritake" and "Japan?" Alternatively, might we conclude that "Noritake collectors" are people who collect post-1921 porcelains marked with the words "Noritake" and "Japan" (rather than "Nippon")? Once again, if you answered "no" to both of these questions, give yourself an A+. In fact, neither of the conclusions entailed by the wording of these questions is valid.

Although it is true, in fact, that most North Americans who define themselves as "Noritake collectors" are only interested in porcelains made by the Noritake Company, they also know that the word "Noritake" was not always a part of backstamps used on many of the porcelains made by the Noritake Company, even for those pieces made after 1921 and destined for export to the United States. Thus, as tempting and as easy as it would be, a "Noritake collector" cannot be defined as one who collects Noritake-marked porcelains, because: 1) not all Noritake-made porcelains were so marked; and 2) many self-described "Noritake collectors" are interested in them. By the same token, it is obvious that one cannot set the scope of a "Noritake book" in these terms; to do so would be to exclude many pieces of interest to the typical "Noritake collector," specifically, pieces marked with the Cherry Blossom backstamp and several others which are discussed in Chapter 3.

At this point, let me present another hypothetical collector. You have not visited this collector's home either, but you know that he or she collects only pieces of porcelain made by the Noritake Company which have the word "Noritake" in the backstamp and which were exported to the United States after 1921. Could you conclude from this information that this person would generally be recognized as a "Noritake collector" and that he or she is one who should probably find a book such as this to be of interest? Again, the answer to each part of this question is "no." Such a person could be collecting Noritake dinnerware, which is for the most part, excluded from this book (the exceptions are pieces in the Azalea, Roseara, and Tree-in-the-Meadow dinnerware patterns which are found in this book).

To review again, we have managed to reach two more conclusions. First, we cannot define "Noritake collectors" simply as people who collect porcelains marked with the word "Noritake," because not all porcelains made by the Noritake Company and of interest to "Noritake collectors" have backstamps which include the word "Noritake." Second, not all those who collect porcelains which are made by the Noritake Company and which are marked as such, are interested in the pieces shown in this book. Moreover, most such (dinnerware) collectors do not define themselves as "Noritake collectors," and if they do, they certainly do not do so in a manner that alludes to the meanings intended by others who use the word and who would be interested in this book.

Earlier, I noted that these issues were linked to "North America" and/or to the "United States." To understand this point, consider yet another hypothetical collector; again, one whose home you have not visited. This person defines him- or herself as a "Noritake collector." When you heard about this person and thought of arranging to see his or her collection, you recalled the above issues and you made some carefully-worded inquiries. For example, you asked if the pieces in the collection were non-dinnerware items marked "Noritake," and if in addition, there were pieces with backstamps which, although without the word "Noritake," were known to be used to mark items made by the Noritake Company. When you heard that the answer to each of these questions was "yes," you arranged to see the collection. Eagerly anticipating a feast for your Art Deco-starved eyes, you find that most of the pieces, although marked "Noritake," are in terms of style, more like pre-1921 "Nippon" pieces.

After some discussion, you discover that this is explained by another of those historical accidents previously discussed. Although prior to 1921, the words "Noritake" and "Japan" were not commonly part of the backstamps of porcelains made for export by the Noritake Company to the United States, this was not true for porcelains made by the Noritake Company which were destined for export to Great Britain. Why this is the case is unclear, because laws comparable to those in effect in the United States in 1921 were not initiated in Great Britain until 1926. The hypothetical collector in the example given happens to have built the collection while living in England but has since moved to the United States. As you discover soon enough, this collector has only a dim understanding of what it means to say that one is a "Nippon collector," or, for that matter, why so many "Nippon collectors" collect porcelains that were not made by the Noritake Company.

So now where are we? I think we can safely say two things at this point. First, we can now say more precisely what it means to be a "Noritake collector;" second, it won't be a simple statement. It will, however, help our effort to create and to justify a statement about the scope of this book.

Provisionally, we may say that a "Noritake collector" is a person who collects non-dinnerware porcelains (except for Azalea, Roseara, and Tree-in-the-Meadow) marked with the word "Noritake" as well as porcelains known, by various methods, to be produced by the Noritake Company, even though the backstamps do not bear the word "Noritake." Because of differences in the laws which had a bearing on both the distribution of these porcelains and decisions regarding the use of the word "Noritake" in the backstamps, some "Noritake collectors" will be oriented primarily to Noritake porcelains made after 1921 and other collectors to Noritake porcelains made after approximately 1908.

Alas, even this definition does not settle all the pertinent matters. To illustrate with one last hypothetical collector: suppose (knowing what you now know) that you have arranged to visit the home of a self-described "Noritake collector" who has assured you, in response to your carefully crafted questions, that he or she collects only post-1908 non-dinnerware Noritake porcelains made for export to the United States or Great Britain and which have backstamps that include the word "Noritake" or backstamps known to be Noritake even if "Noritake" does not appear. You arrive and find that, although this collector did answer honestly and correctly given the facts and the wording of your questions, that the collection is unlike anything you have seen before. Rather than the bright, multicolored bowls, perfume bottles, and tea sets from the 1908 to 1938 period you are familiar with, you instead see many strikingly different pure white figurines (horses, dogs, among many others), bright red figurines (mostly of fish), and variously colored porcelain eggs and hearts (for Easter and Valentine's Day, respectively)!

Again, upon inquiry, you learn that this "Noritake collector" is, as had been claimed, only interested in post-1908 Noritake-marked non-dinnerware collectibles but what you did not know, because you had no idea you needed to ask, is that this collector is only interested in pieces made by the Noritake Company *after* 1945. Does this mean that we must set a date range for "Noritake collectors?" Should the date range be, for example, 1908 to the start of World War II? In fact, many self-

defined "Noritake collectors" today see it this way, but this view also appears to be changing.

I did say it would be complicated, did I not? Be assured then, dear reader, that we are near the end of this saga, although not because all the relevant issues have been raised and the pertinent questions answered. Enough have been answered, however, to permit me to proceed to the "bottom line" for this subject–namely, how all of this information bears on the scope of this book. This is, after all, one of the primary reasons for initially raising the question. Thus, the scope of this book may be described as follows.

Included in this book are the following kinds of *non-dinnerware* porcelains (with the exception of Azalea, Roseara, and Tree-in-the-Meadow dinnerware patterns) made and decorated by the Noritake Company or its approved subcontractors:

1) those pieces exported from Japan to Great Britain (and other parts of the former "British Empire") after approximately 1908 and up to the present which bear backstamps with the word "Noritake" or which have backstamps known to show that the piece was made and decorated after 1908 by the Noritake Company and/or its approved subcontractors.

2) those pieces exported from Japan to the United States after 1921 and up to the present day which bear backstamps with the word "Noritake" or backstamps known to indicate that the piece was made and decorated after 1921 by the Noritake Company and/or its approved subcontractors.

3) Noritake-made and backstamped porcelains intended originally for use in Japan, although none have been included in this book. Potential examples would include the dinnerware designed by Frank Lloyd Wright in the 1920s for the Imperial Hotel in Tokyo or certain unusual souvenir pieces distributed by the Noritake Company for use on various special occasions.

Excluded from this book are the following kinds of Noritake Company porcelains:

1) dinnerware (except Azalea, Roseara, and Tree-in-the-Meadow patterns)

2) pieces with backstamps which include the word "Nippon" (unless it is part of the phrase "Nippon Toki Kaisha" which means, essentially, Japanese Ceramics Company), even if the word "Noritake" is also a part of it

3) pieces made by the Noritake Company but which were exported undecorated with the expectation that these would be decorated outside of Japan either by hobbyist decorators or by non-Noritake companies (e.g., Picard).

All of this said, when the term "Noritake collectors" is used in this book, it may be understood most simply to refer to people who collect some or all of the types of porcelains included in this book.

Chapter 2

The Noritake Company & Noritake Collecting: History and Trends

This is not a book about all items ever created by the Noritake Company. It's a good thing, too. Such a book could easily be 10 times the size of this one! Although not widely known to collectors and consumers of Noritake china, the Noritake Company today produces much more than "dishes." This fact has been true for decades. Corporate diversification over the years has been such that china and other "tabletop" products account for only approximately 33% of the Noritake Company's annual sales total of 100 billion yen. Various industrial products account for the remainder of the company's production. For example, the Noritake Company is now and for some years has been one of the world's leading manufacturers of industrial grinding wheels. It also produces a variety of sophisticated electronic items. Today, the company's products, including their well-known porcelains and other tabletop wares, are not manufactured only in Japan. The pieces are also made in Germany, Ireland, Sri Lanka, the Philippines, and Singapore.

Still, when most people hear the name "Noritake," they think of "Japanese dishes." There are several good reasons for this. First, few individuals must purchase or know anything about industrial-grade grinding wheels. Second, the company's international reputation was established early in this century when it began to export huge quantities of high-quality but affordable porcelain dinnerware. In terms of volume, the Noritake Company has been and it is today, at or very near the top of the list of companies worldwide which produce such dinnerware. So established is this link between "Noritake" and "Japanese dishes" that it is certain that every "Noritake collector" has had to explain to a friend that the items, such as those shown here, really were produced in Japan by "that dinnerware company." To them, this is "news," just as to many Noritake collectors it continues to be "news" that the company they seem to know so well also produces an extensive line of high-quality crystal stemware, stainless and silver flatware, saws, and electronic subway signs.

In this chapter, I discuss the history of the Noritake Company and also offer comments about stylistic trends in the porcelains produced by the company, especially prior to 1941. I also discuss briefly how the fancy line porcelains of Morimura Bros., Inc. were brought to consumers in all parts of the United States, showing some unusual and rare Noritake-related collectibles which have been seen by very few collectors.

History

Although it is easy to do otherwise, one should take note of facts beyond those indicating size or annual sales when discussing corporations. The Noritake Company, for example, is far more than "big." It is an old and highly respected company. What we currently know as the "Noritake Company"–a name not adopted officially until 1981–was founded on January 1st of 1904. The company's roots go back much further, however.

A key early date is 1839 (unless stated otherwise, all the names, dates, places, and key developments in Noritake Company history mentioned in this essay are drawn from various Noritake Company sources, including their book *Early Noritake* and books by Donahue, Kottler and Van Patten; all are listed in the bibliography). That was the birth year of Ichizaemon

Morimura, the person who, less than two decades later, would start a business that by 1904 would become the corporation which has grown into the Noritake Company of today (see photo 2.1). Young Ichizaemon Morimura's parents were successful merchants, which likely contributed to his desire to succeed in business, although there was far more to it than that.

A vital part of the story may be picked up in 1854. In that year, when the Morimura brothers were teenagers, Commodore Matthew Perry made his fateful arrival in Japan. He brought many things with him, including heavily armed ships. Moreover, in his baggage was a letter for the Emperor of Japan from President Franklin Pierce. In it, the American President raised an issue that many today will think familiar. He wanted Japan to open its borders to trade. After protracted negotiations, the Emperor of Japan did agree to open the borders of Japan to trade and accordingly, in 1858, Japan signed the "Friendship and Commerce Treaty," not only with the United States but also Russia, the Netherlands, Great Britain, and France. In response, in 1859, an official Japanese trade delegation was sent to the United States. One member of it was Ichizaemon Morimura, then only 20 years of age.

Perry's "visit" to Japan was one of a series of events culminating in what is referred to as the "decline and fall" of Japan's "Feudal" era, a period dominated by powerful local rulers known as *Shoguns*. By 1868, however, this era, known as the "Shogunate" period, came to an end; this end was symbolized most dramatically by moving the imperial capital of Japan from Kyoto to Tokyo. With this move, the Meiji dynasty was firmly established. This also marked the beginning of radical change for many Japanese, including a complete reshaping of the commercial sector of Japanese society.

Morimura and his business partners were among many who were well positioned to take advantage of the opportunities brought about by these changes. For example, by 1876, Ichizaemon's 23-year-old brother had moved to New York City to establish The Hinode Company. This company received and sold, as retailer, regular shipments of Japanese curios, paper lanterns, and china wares and was very successful. In 1877 or 1878 (Company sources differ), a store was opened on more fashionable Sixth Avenue. This successful export-import-retailing business might have remained unchanged for many years except that Morimura and some co-workers decided to attend the Paris Exhibition of 1878 (an event of interest also because it presages a similar event occurring about 50 years later in Paris, which again will significantly impact the Noritake Company).

At this "World's Fair," Morimura saw and was impressed by the fine, richly decorated porcelains produced in Europe. In 1883, one of the Morimura brothers did something which fundamentally changed the fledgling company: he sent a coffee cup to Japan. This was not just any coffee cup; it was a French-made cup of high-quality, hard porcelain. Within a short time, the Morimura Group (known as Morimura Gumi in Japan) was devoted to acquiring and developing the skills necessary to produce such high-quality porcelains in Japan, for export principally to the United States.

This led the Morimura Gumi to send Japanese artisans to Europe to acquire certain essential skills pertaining to the manufacture and decoration of fine porcelains. It also led to the closing of the Hinode retail company in New York and establishing in its place, in 1879, a new porcelain-manufacturing and wholesale company, called Morimura Bros. and Co., as it was known in New York (the other five founders, besides Ichizaemon himself, are shown in photos 2.2 through 2.6). Morimura and/or others from the Noritake Company sought ideas and information from many sources. For example, in 1893, company members attended the World's Fair in Chicago. In 1900, they went to the World Exposition in Paris, and in 1903, they visited Austria's world famous Victoria Ceramics Factory, headed by Louis Rosenfeld. Although details are not available, it is certain that many useful techniques were learned which enabled the Morimura Gumi to prosper with much hard work.

The pace of development and change quickened after construction of the factory at the town of Nagoya in 1904 (photos 2.7 through 2.9), by what had become "Nippon Toki Gomei Kaisha," a name which means, in essence, Japanese Ceramics Company. The site was selected in part because of the huge supplies of kaolin (a type of clay vital to the manufacture of fine porcelain) nearby. Initially, dinnerware porcelains were produced at this factory for the domestic market, including the Imperial household. According to Donahue, the prince who would become Japan's Emperor Taisho paid a visit to the factory in 1910 and ordered dinnerware on several occasions, as did many of Japan's well-traveled elites. The factory also supplied dinnerware for the Japanese Navy, and by 1911, the company was selling dinnerware in the country's main department stores.

One of the most important developments in the entire history of the company occurred in 1914. It was then that porcelain dinnerware pattern D1441, named "Sedan," was exported to the United States. The plates were white with a pale cream-colored border spotted with small clusters of delicate flowers. With this export began a tradition that continues to this day: the Noritake Company's world leadership in the manufacture and export of fine porcelain dinnerware. During this time, however, the company also produced what they refer to as their "fancy line" (*Early Noritake*, p.12). These products were inspired by visits to the World Exhibitions and Fairs and visiting factories, such as those of Louis Rosenfeld.

Prior to 1921, these intricately decorated fancy line pieces (as well as the dinnerware) exported to the United States bore backstamps which included the word "Nippon," an Anglicized version of the Japanese word for "Japan." Between 1890 and 1921, all products imported into the United States from foreign countries were required to have the name of the country affixed to them. Fancy-line pieces in Art Nouveau styles and other pieces reminiscent of earlier 19th century Belle-Epoque European design predominated during this time (these breathtakingly beautiful pieces are best documented in the book *Early Noritake* published by the Noritake Company and in Van Patten's four books on "Nippon" collectibles, which are mentioned in the bibliography).

These stylistic trends would change, however, for reasons similar to those which influenced the company nearly 50 years earlier (i.e., the International Exposition in Paris). Held in 1925, this previously scheduled Exposition had been delayed by World War I. The Exposition, the "Exposition Internationale des Arts Décoratifs et Industriels Modernes," which has been the subject of much discussion and debate, presented a huge array of decorative and artistic products in styles which are known as "Art Deco" today. The Noritake Company soon began producing its "fancy line" items in this style. This shift had been presaged by products exported just before and after the legally

mandated shift in 1921, to the use of the word "Japan" in place of the word "Nippon" to indicate the country of origin.

In particular, the company began producing wares with (as Kottler puts it) "a more colorful range of overglazes and lusters." By 1921, the lusterware "era" was underway, an era that was made all the more exuberant when the company fully absorbed the impact of the 1925 Paris Exposition. The transfer of design motifs and ideas to the Noritake factory at Nagoya was the responsibility of the design staff at the offices in New York. Glimpses into this part of the production process were provided to Howard Kottler, a pioneering collector of Art Deco Noritake porcelains, through interviews with Cele Shapiro. Ms. Shapiro worked in the New York offices of Morimura Bros. from 1914 to 1941 (see Kottler's essay "The Search for Noritake," pp.31-36 of *Noritake Art Deco Porcelains*; see bibliography for details). Ms. Shapiro was secretary to Charles Kaiser, the manager of Morimura Bros. and the head of the company sales department. In short, she was familiar with the daily workings in that office and all over the country.

The leading figure in the design department, according to Kottler's interviews with Shapiro (p.34), was an Englishman, Cyril Leigh. Little is known about the details of the design process, except that it was very successful. It is evident, from the Noritake designs and motifs of this period, that the artists who worked with Leigh were influenced by virtually all major themes and artists of the Art Deco era. Many of the florals and geometric designs seem to speak to and of the generally vibrant tone of the style, while some of the "lady" motifs were clearly inspired by specific graphic and fashion design statements published in magazines of the era, such as *Vogue* or *Vanity Fair*. In a few instances, the original artist can even be specified. Erté was one of these, according to Ronny Cohen (pp.27-28 of the Kottler book) and another was Homer Conant, an illustrator who created prints which were distributed widely in the mid 1920s (photo 2.10 shows a well-known Noritake plate against one of the Conant prints associated with the 1924 hit Broadway musical, "Madame Pompadour").

Knowing this, some collectors have begun to look for and accumulate examples of designs found on 1920s Noritake items which appear in other settings as well (e.g., photos 2.11 through 2.15, all created by Margaret Anderson). Clearly, the designers in New York were creatures of their time. As pointed out in the book *Early Noritake* (p. 11), however, the flow of inspiration was never simply in one direction. "It was not simply the East importing the modern culture from the West; the West too was influenced greatly from its encounter with the East."

The Great Depression of the late 20s and early 30s hit Japan and the Noritake Company hard. Although the company continued to export porcelains to the United States during this time, the designs may have been toned down, at least according to Kottler (p.56). If that is the case and given that there were no Art Deco designs on Noritake pieces prior to 1925 (the year of the Paris Exhibition), the bulk of the items in this book which are distinctly Art Deco in appearance were produced during a 5-year period (for a detailed discussion on Art Deco Noritake, see my essay in Van Patten's second series book on Noritake collectibles). I think you will agree it is nothing short of phenomenal that the Noritake Company could produce such a stunningly diverse and high-quality array of porcelains in so short a time.

This production would come to a thundering halt by 1941, of course, with the outbreak of hostilities involving not only Japan and the United States, but the entire world. The New York offices were closed (although they would reopen after the

2.1 Ichizaemon Morimura (1839-1919), founder of Morimura Gumi and ultimately the Noritake Company.

2.3 Saneyoshi Hirose (1844-1924).

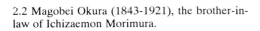

2.2 Magobei Okura (1843-1921), the brother-in-law of Ichizaemon Morimura.

2.4 Yasutaka Murai (1854-1936).

2.5 Kazuchika Okura (1875-1955), the son of Magobei Morimura and the first President of the Company.

2.7 Noritake Company plant under construction in 1904 near Nagoya.

2.8 Company officials at the Nagoya Plant under construction in 1904.

2.6 Koraro Asukai (1867-1927).

2.9 View of the Nagoya factory in 1905.

2.12 Noritake ashtray and a crepe paper package with similar motifs.

2.10 Noritake plaque with motif that echos a 1920s print by Homer Conant.

2.11 Noritake tea tile and part of a paper bridge tally set with similar motifs.

2.13 Noritake napkin rings and a bridge tally set with similar motifs.

2.15 Noritake sugar shaker (muffineer; *right*) and a perfume bottle (*left*) with an "architectural" feel similar to the Chrysler Building (widely regarded as an Art Deco masterpiece).

2.14 Noritake bowl with figural handle, playing card and a non-Noritake ceramic figurine with similar motifs.

war). During the war, the company in Japan ceased production of tableware and concentrated on the making of grinding wheels. The size of the staff decreased significantly, especially toward the end of the war. After the war, the company was forced to divest some of its subsidiaries. It also was obligated to produce dinnerware for the occupation forces under rather adverse conditions, leading the company to use a backstamp, for a period, with the words "Rose China" instead of the company name.

Slowly the factories were rebuilt, and soon delicate, exquisite porcelains were being produced, reminiscent of those which had given the company its well-deserved reputation prior to the war. Chief among these pieces were the bone china figurines. Thanks to information supplied by the Noritake Company, many of these figurines can now be dated with some precision. The earliest pieces for which I have reliable information were made in 1946, which gives some hint as to the strength of the desire felt by workers to create a product of truly timeless beauty. Several of these fine early pieces can be found in Chapter F of this book.

Trends

Now we have some idea of how the Noritake Company moved the porcelains to its New York warehouses. The next question is: how did these porcelains get to the consumer, especially when the consumers were scattered all over the country? The answer: *salesmen*. The Noritake Company was no longer in the retail business in New York. To sell their porcelains, the Noritake Company had to rely upon a fairly sizeable group of salesmen who visited store after store, seeking retail outlets for Noritake wares. These stores ranged from the most elegant to the most modest. Examples of the latter may be seen in Photos 2.16 and 2.17, which are postcards from the early years of this century. One photo (2.16) shows what is referred to as a "Japanese Exposition" held in Venice, California; the other photo (2.17) from the same era, as may be judged by the lamps for sale in the picture (the card is postmarked March 7, 1909), and possibly from the same area, shows a store featuring an expansive array of what appears to be Japanese-made ceramics.

For store owners, the question that remained, given the scale of the Noritake Company production, is what to order. It seems there were at least two ways to answer this question. First, some salesmen carried "salesmen sample books" with them (photos 2.18 and 2.19 show such a book, closed and open to the first page). These books varied in size. The cover of the book shown in the photo is 12" h x 8.25" w. The pages in it are approximately 11.5" h x 7.5" w (including the binding strip), and the book is 3" thick. In other words, there are scores of pages in it.

Far less is known about these books than we wish. The term *salesman book* is derived from the fact that, on the inside margins (or binding strip) of each page, normally hidden by the binding (typically loose-leaf) are the words "NOT FOR SALE. SALESMAN'S USE. MADE IN JAPAN." These pages were not printed. Rather, each page is an original work of art, hand painted by factory artisans who were copying a master design, which in many cases was originally produced in the offices of Morimura Brothers in New York City (see photos 2.20 through 2.37; photos 2.20 through 2.25 are from the book shown in photo 2.18, and items 2.26 through 2.37, which are loose pages, are from the Buonafede collection). It is not known how many of these books were created. So far, only a few have been discovered in the United States. The Noritake Company also has some in its possession.

The page usually does not show an entire piece (the sample of pages shown here is intentionally unrepresentative in this respect). Because the emphasis was to recreate the design exactly, it makes sense that only portions would be reproduced, while still giving an adequate sense of how the finished piece would look. On most of these pages, there are various numbers and letters and what appears to be a Japanese character. I do not know what these characters may have indicated. It does seem that the numbers and/or letters might be pattern or design codes, but because there are sometimes several of these numbers on the same page, this hypothesis (although perhaps not incorrect) is probably much too simple.

For most collectors, these design pages are almost as exciting to see and own as the Noritake pieces themselves, partly because these paper items are intrinsically more fragile and likely to be destroyed than the pieces themselves. Whatever the reason, it is certain that these pages are precious to all collectors. You are invited to see how many of the designs shown here you can find on pieces shown elsewhere in this book (and in other books on Noritake collectibles).

Salesmen were important to the company, but trade publications provided another avenue for exposure. An example of such a publication was the *Crockery & Glass Journal*. Shown in photos 2.38 and 2.39 are the front and back covers of the "Holiday Number" of December 18, 1924, which features a beautiful ad for Morimura Bros., complete with an "M-in-Wreath" on the tablecloth (something else for dedicated Noritake collectors to look for). Although the graphics of the front cover tend to hold the attention, the back cover is just as interesting, because the pieces shown there were presumably among the more recent additions to the Noritake Company fancy line. If this is so, it would enable collectors to assign production dates to their pieces–something many collectors would like to do.

Several pieces shown in that back-cover ad will, I suspect, be familiar to many collectors and dealers. For example, consider the nut bowl in the lower left, the cigarette set near the upper left, the condiment set and powder jar just across from it, and the beehive honey pot at the top of the page. Are any of these pieces in your collection or your booth at the mall? If so, you now know a bit more about the piece than you did. Look carefully because decorations and designs on these pieces may be similar to but not identical to the pieces you have.

Now that stores have their wares, is anything known about the patrons who bought them and their reasons for buying? One clue comes from what is described as the "Larkin connection" (see Barbara Soper's essay in Van Patten 1984, pp.30-32). For a few decades at the end of the nineteenth and the beginning of the twentieth centuries, the Larkin Company was an extremely successful soap, ceramics, and mail-order company based in Buffalo, New York. In the early decades of this century, many Americans obtained the Noritake Company's Tree-in-the-Meadow, Azalea, and Roseara patterns both by direct purchase from the Larkin Company or as premiums "earned" by other purchases. This connection did not focus on dinnerware alone. A book on the Larkin Company by Walter Ayars contains page after page of Larkin display ads. With a bit of careful searching, the eager Noritake collector can find many ads in the Ayars book with some of their favorite fancy line items: pieces ranging from elegant figural dresser dolls to bold Art Deco napkin rings.

Another clue turns up in the anecdotes Noritake collectors frequently tell when asked how they began collecting "that stuff." Many collectors began after inheriting a piece of fancy line (sometimes dinnerware) Noritake porcelain from a relative who received it as a wedding present or holiday gift. From this information, we may learn several things. In some instances, we gain more precise dates for a motif or blank or a sense of how special these pieces may have been at the time. Two pieces documented in this way are shown here.

Photo 2.40 shows a fairly elaborate Noritake salt and pepper set in the original box with the gift card still enclosed. On it is written, "To dear Hattie: wishing you a Merry Christmas and Happy 1928." Obviously, this collection was given as a present for Christmas 1927, and thus, tells us that this set (which bears backstamp MIJ.0) was available at least by that date, 70 years ago. The other item shown here (photo 2.41) is a simple lemon plate, made far more special to collectors by virtue of the words taped to the back (photo 2.42): Wedding gift to Esther and Art LeMay, June 1929. Obviously, in addition to the date, we can see that even something as seemingly plain as a lemon plate was seen as special enough to be given as a wedding present.

Prior to 1921, the reputation of the Noritake Company rested on at least three key factors. Noritake "fancy line" wares were: 1) high-quality porcelains, that 2) were affordably priced, which 3) had stylish and exquisite hand-applied decorations. These pieces, in both shape and applied decoration, predominately exhibited Arts and Crafts, Art Nouveau, and other earlier European styles and motifs. Hand work was the norm. The colors on these pieces covered the full spectrum. Many pieces, especially those with an Art Nouveau influence, were decorated in bright greens, lush lavenders, and dramatic pinks. One marvels at the grace and subtlety of the pieces produced prior to 1921. Even more impressive is the effort *lavished* on the decoration of the pieces: thousands of beads of clay overlay applied drop by drop; hundreds of shades of paint blended by thousands of brush strokes; ounces (seemingly) of gold on pieces which, in comparison with what would soon become the norm, can only be described as huge. The results were and still are awesome.

Even so, except for the extensive use of gold, most of the fancy line pieces prior to 1921 tended to be relatively quiet, warm, and soft in character and even somber in tone. These qualities were achieved by the widespread use of matte finishes and warm colors: an abundance of browns and yellows, as well as warm and subtle shades of "cool" colors, such as blue and green. Common motifs also contribute to this restful, serene feeling: sandy desert vistas, dark woodland haunts, faint mountain landscapes, cozy thatch-roofed cottages, wistful harvest scenes, mysterious stone-colored castle ruins, dark and creaky windmills against purple and brown skies, still lakes with swans at rest, swans in graceful flight against brown, reed-clogged ponds, fat cattle grazing in autumn glens, birds in pale yellows and warm whites, monks in brown robes, fishermen in tan slickers, mottled fall leaves, walnuts, deer antlers, lions, dogs, monkeys, horses, owls, racoons . . . all in brown.

Although the use of a limited (while still diverse) array of mass-produced blanks gives a unity to this variety, the amazing thing about these pieces is that most of the decorations were applied by hand. Each sky, each tree, each leaf is unique. Photos 2.43 and 2.44 show two Noritake plates which nicely exemplify the warmth and calmness I have described (these have backstamp 27.0). Although far simpler than many pre-1921 Noritake pieces, these feelings are fostered in the two pieces, as in thousands of others, by the careful selection of colors and design elements. By briefly viewing the photos at a distance, one may conclude that they are alike (and in a sense, they are).

Upon closer inspection (photos 2.45 and 2.46), however, it is clear that there are rather striking differences to the pieces. On one piece, the ridge of the cottage roof comes to a point at one end; on the other, the roof seems to droop at the bottom corner. On one piece, the windows appear similar to the portholes of a ship; on the other, the windows are nearly square and appear to be shuttered. Many other differences are just as striking. Compare the smoothness of the shoreline, the width of the path, the angle of the tree, the shape of the shrubs, and the location of the clouds. Many other interesting points of contrast can be found, I am sure.

By approximately 1921, the color palette on Noritake fancy-line pieces began to brighten considerably, along with (not entirely coincidentally, in my view) trends emerging in the bright, "roaring" economy of the post-war decade. Prior to 1921, the Noritake Company did produce pieces using finishing glazes which resulted in bright, metallic, high-sheen surfaces. There are a few pre-1921 Noritake pieces which feature these luster glazes. For example, the cup in photo 2.47 has an "M-in-Wreath" backstamp with the word "Nippon" instead of "Japan," indicating clearly that this piece was made prior to 1921. Even so, the surface is not the usual porcelain white but, instead, a beautiful, bluish shade of iridescent mother-of-pearl luster (and a bright blue band around the rim). This is an interesting transitional piece, a hint of changes to come, as it were–changes even the Noritake Company did not anticipate fully at the time (indeed, no one did).

Photos 2.48 and 2.49 show two lemon plates, from different collections in Seattle, that also are interesting transitional pieces. As with the plates shown in the above-mentioned photos (in one Seattle collection), if the two pieces are studied a bit, it becomes obvious that the two hand-painted scenes are strikingly different. What is more notable, however, is the use and effect of the blue-luster finish on these pieces. The matte-finished painted scenes are still somber, yet pleasant, but luster rims give each piece as a whole what can only be described as a "brighter" look which, in turn, usually fosters a corresponding shift in the viewer's mood (tiny as the shift may be). (Note: I am *not* saying, in making this comparison, that bright is good and somber is bad. These contrasting colors and finishes are just *different*. On some days, I may prefer one to the other for various reasons; indeed, I may prefer one to the other generally. But saying this is only a subjective aesthetic judgment involving preference and a highly personal one at that. This is not an objective fact entailing moral worth, as would be implied by flatly using the words "good" and "bad" in such a context.)

For nearly 4 years at the beginning of the 1920s, the Noritake Company exported to the United States a new "Made in Japan" fancy line of porcelain. According to the book *Early Noritake*, the fancy line was an adjunct to its dinnerware mainstay. These items were still handpainted, at least in part, but in contrast to the Nippon-era items, they are literally and figuratively highlighted by the addition of bright, particularly blue-colored, luster glazes. Does this mark the onset of a different style? It all depends on the definition of the term "*style*." As noted previously, however, motifs play at least as much a role in creating the style or "look" of a piece as do colors.

We must inquire what the motifs were during this brief pre-1925 era. The answer, in essence, is that *the motifs remain within the range* developed during the first 15 to 20 years of the century. There still are many golden meadows, quiet ponds, cozy cottages, sitting swans, and pleasant flowers; there are also more than a few mallards rising gracefully, creeks flowing lazily, and cows grazing contentedly. Curiously, for yet unknown reasons, the range of motifs is much more limited and the physical scale of Noritake fancy-line pieces had diminished considerably by the early 1920s. Gone are the magnificent 18", 21", and 24" "palace urns." Gold is used sparingly, cobalt blues are no longer used, and many seemingly inexhaustible design themes suddenly ceased.

By 1925 or so, however, this trend changes abruptly. What was merely hinted at in the two lemon plates previously discussed is about to become a full-blown trend–a fact amply demonstrated in the pages of Part Two. The year 1925 is pivotal in this regard because that is the year of the Paris Exposition, which presented to the world various movements in the decorative arts which had been in development since the onset of the century. Since around 1966, these movements have been grouped under the single and somewhat troublesome term "Art Deco."

There are many ways to describe the change that took place. To me, it is similar to the conversion from silent films to "talkie" movies, from black-and-white to color television, from the waltz to the Charleston, or from folk songs to jazz. However described, it is clear that after 1925 the Noritake fancy line gained a new vigor in colors, motifs, and blanks. Wide-eyed clowns, sophisticated ladies, golfing ladies, cigarette-smoking ladies, ladies applying makeup, ladies wearing the latest fashions, top-hatted gents, salt and pepper shakers in the shape of townhouses, wacky figural birds, abstract, off-color florals, romantic cottages no longer beside mind-numbing lakes but sitting at the edge of well-defined roads in the midst of exotic flowers and giant stylized trees. There are wild, zig zag-filled geometric patterns and piece after piece in a veritable rainbow of lusters: blue, tan, green, yellow, orange, pink, and mother-of-pearl in several tints. Brown tones are so rare during this period that the few pieces on which they predominate stand out when they are seen.

The character of the post-1925 fancy line works could not be more different from those made prior to this watershed year.

The depression years, however, which were solidly entrenched by the early 1930s, brought this design explosion to an end. How rapidly, we do not know. We are told that the backstamps used during the 1920s continued to be in use until 1941, when the New York office of Morimura Brothers was closed. What we do not know is how many designs were first introduced during the depths of the depression–i.e., beginning in the early 1930s. It may be presumed that, although the fancy line continued to be produced during these bleak years, the pieces must have been less vigorous, stylistically.

The next major event (and nearly the last we will consider in this essay) was the second of the two world wars in this century. As previously noted, this event brought the production of Noritake porcelains to a complete halt for many years. For some people, it did much more than this. The war led countless Americans, Canadians, Australians, and English, in a fit of patriotic fervor, to dispose of their Japanese-made porcelains–a conclusion based both on anecdote and on the fact that so many pieces of Noritake have been found with either the backstamp sanded off or the word "Japan" removed.

These vandalistic acts precede an even longer post-war period (circa 1945 to 1975) when it seems almost nobody wanted "that Japanese junk." "You couldn't give it away," say dealers who have been in the business since the early 1970s. Indeed, all collectors who began their search prior to 1990 have encountered more than a few dealers who would ridicule anyone foolish enough to express an interest in 20th-century, mass-produced Japanese porcelains. This is an attitude which, if encountered today, provokes amazement in collectors and informed dealers because they *know* now that they were wise to invest their time and hard-earned income by collecting and dealing Noritake collectibles from *all* time periods. It is this most recent trend in Noritake collecting that is celebrated here. Enjoy!

2.16 Japanese Exposition held in Venice, California.

2.17 Interior of store with what appears to be extensive Japanese ceramic merchandise.

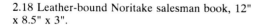

2.18 Leather-bound Noritake salesman book, 12" x 8.5" x 3".

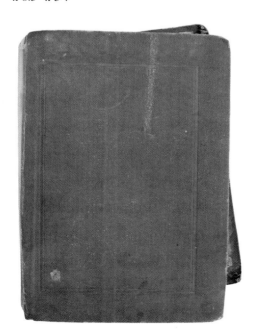

2.19 Noritake salesmen's book shown in 2.18 opened to the first page.

2.20 Page from the salesmen's book shown in 2.18.

2.21 Page from the salesmen's book shown in 2.18.

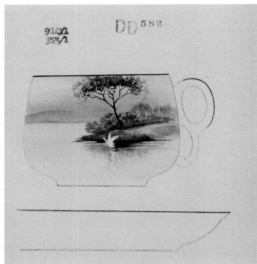

2.24 Page from the salesmen's book shown in 2.18.

2.25 Page from the salesmen's book shown 2.18.

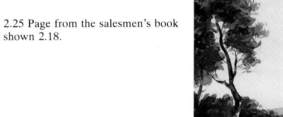

2.22 Page from the salesmen's book shown in 2.18.

2.23 Page from the salesmen's book shown in 2.18.

2.26 Page from a Noritake salesmen's book.

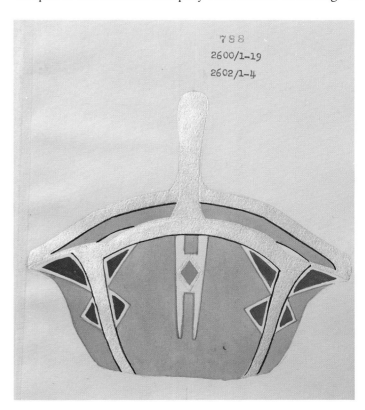

2.28 Page from a Noritake salesmen's book.

2.29 Page from a Noritake salesmen's book.

2.27 Page from a Noritake salesmen's book.

2.30 Page from a Noritake salesmen's book.

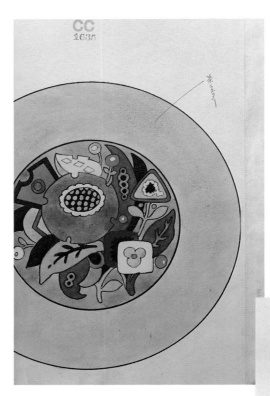

2.33 Page from a Noritake salesmen's book.

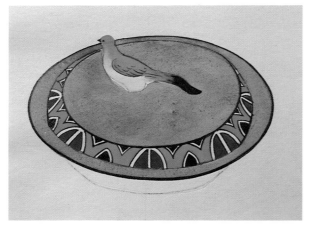

2.31 Page from a Noritake salesmen's book.

2.34 Page from a Noritake salesmen's book.

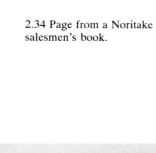

2.32 Page from a Noritake salesmen's book.

2.35 Page from a Noritake salesmen's book.

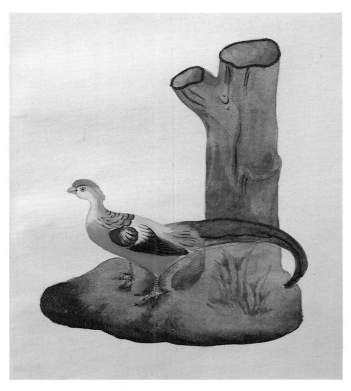

2.37 Page from a Noritake salesmen's book.

2.36 Page from a Noritake salesmen's book.

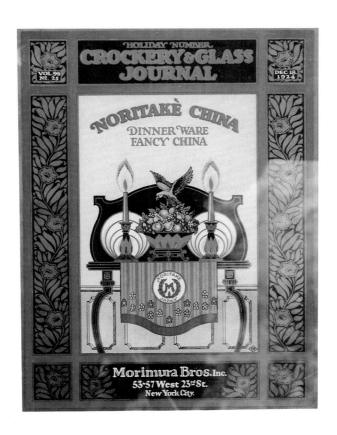

2.38 Front cover of *Crockery and Glass Journal*, December 18, 1924.

2.39 Back cover of *Crockery and Glass Journal*, December 18, 1924.

2.41 Noritake lemon plate.

2.42 Reverse of lemon plate in 2.41 showing the tag which states "Wedding gift to Esther and Art LeMay, June 1929."

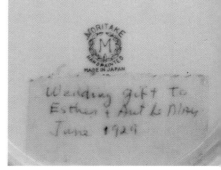

2.43 Noritake plate with painted scene.

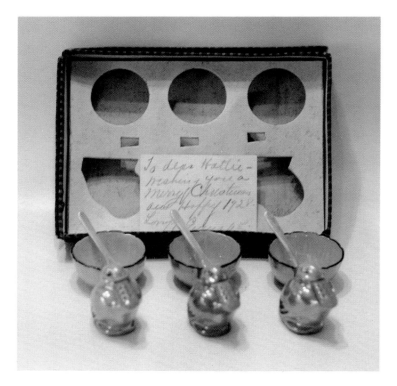

2.40 Noritake salt and pepper set with gift card that reads, "To dear Hattie---Wishing you a Merry Christmas and Happy 1928."

2.47 Noritake made "Nippon"-marked cup in blue-tinted, mother-of-pearl luster.

2.44 Noritake plate with painted scene.

2.45 Close-up of the scene in 2.43.

2.48 Noritake lemon plate with painted scene and blue luster.

2.49 Noritake lemon plate with painted scene and blue luster.

2.46 Close-up of the scene in 2.44.

Chapter 3

Noritake Backstamps: Their Names & Numbers

Because this chapter is more technical and somewhat longer than the others, I begin with a brief overview consisting of the following five short paragraphs. Upon reading them, you should be able to decide quickly which parts of this chapter you will either want or need to read.

Overview

Previous researchers have identified well over 100 "Noritake" backstamps. Although others continue to be discovered, the pace of discovery is slower now than 20 years ago. When Noritake backstamps were first collected, it was impossible to give much structure to the lists or indicate which backstamps were most important to the collector or dealer. Appropriately enough, the emphasis was placed on cataloging and assigning dates where possible to any backstamp discovered–a demanding task in itself. The four published lists of Noritake backstamps differ considerably in content, and some known Noritake backstamps are not found in any of the lists. The lists present other difficulties as well.

Therefore, a new system for numbering backstamps was developed. Although it too is certainly imperfect, this system was designed to solve three existing problems. This system is meant to be: 1) *very* easy to use; 2) able to accommodate new backstamps when discovered; and 3) indicative of chronology without requiring that the user remember numerous arcane details about either the backstamp or the numbering system. The system also was designed to be similar in certain ways to the best known of the several existing numbering systems. For the rationale of this system, see pp. 30-34.

Before discussing this new system, I present information about two of the more important Noritake backstamps. First, support is given, despite lingering doubt in some quarters, for the belief that the "Cherry Blossom" backstamp is a "Noritake" backstamp, albeit one which does not bear the company name. Second, interpretative and other comments are offered about the Komaru group of backstamps–marks which are commonly but incorrectly known as "spoke," "wheel," or "spider" backstamps. For details on each, see pp.28-30.

At the end of this chapter (see pp.38-41) are color photos of the specific kinds and nearly all the varieties of backstamps mentioned in Part Two of this book (the few omitted varieties differ only in color from the specific kinds shown). There is also a table listing descriptions of the specific kinds of backstamps. These descriptions are sequenced using the backstamp numbers which designate backstamps in this book. Also provided are the corresponding backstamp numbers used in the other published systems, and information about the *approximate* age of these marks, if known.

At various points throughout this chapter, it is suggested that the overall importance of the backstamps has been greatly exaggerated. This is ironic for several reasons, not least being that (as is common with technical matters) it takes more time to carefully and thoughtfully discuss the relevant issues than one would hope. With this in mind, a simple, practical guide to key backstamps in this field and a summary of their designations in captions is presented in the introduction of Part Two (pp. 42-43). With the summary alone, materials in Part Two of this book can be easily understood.

How many backstamps are there?

Over the years, the Noritake Company has used scores of backstamps. To the best of my knowledge, no one today knows how many were used, and in all likelihood, no single person has ever known. The Noritake Company has had no need to publish extensively on the subject, nor has it done so. In a small pamphlet available from the Noritake museum, only 35 backstamps are shown–20 of which are still in use! In Donahue's pioneering book, *Noritake Collectibles*, published in 1979, 57 backstamps are depicted. In the second volume of Joan Van Patten's *The Collector's Encyclopedia of Noritake,* published in 1994, she catalogs 99 backstamps, 2 more than her previous 1984 book on the same subject. In Alden and Richardson's book *Early Noritake China: An Identification and Value Guide to Tableware Patterns*, published in 1987, more than 150 different Noritake backstamps are highlighted. Although there is quite a bit of overlap in these lists, each list contains backstamps not included in one, or sometimes all, of the other publications. Moreover, there are a few backstamps that have been omitted from all three of the extensive non-corporate sources.

I think the overall gain from catalogs with scores of backstamps can be questioned. Many people are more likely to be daunted than intrigued when encountering pages of black-and-white drawings or photographs of backstamps, especially when many of them appear virtually alike. This seems true not only for most beginning collectors but also for many seasoned veterans. It certainly would appear true for those who consult these books infrequently.

How can someone master such a diverse array of arcane markings? More to the point, *is this necessary* to become a successful collector or dealer? The answer is a classic of the "bad news/good news" genre. The "bad news" is that it would be extremely difficult for most of us to learn the catalog number associated with every Noritake backstamp. One may just as well decide to learn Japanese, since it would be probably no more difficult and certainly more rewarding.

The "good news" is that *one needn't learn the numbers of all these backstamps!* Doing so (unlike learning Japanese) has virtually *no* payoff whatsoever. Why? Because, very few of the backstamps appearing in books have been found on the porcelains shown in this or in similar books. This means that only a few of the many known Noritake backstamps occur with any frequency on the items collected by people identified as "Noritake collectors" (see pp. 7-9 in Chapter 1 for more details on who "Noritake collectors" are).

To give credibility to what many see as a surprising claim, consider the following facts about backstamps recorded for non-dinnerware items shown in the numbered color "plates" of the two Van Patten books on Noritake collectibles. Of the approximately 1536 pieces presented therein, I found only 37 with backstamps which were not variants of the backstamp to which Van Patten assigned the number "27." In other words, more than 97% of all the non-dinnerware pieces in those books have the number "27" backstamp or some variant of it.

The trend is even more striking if one deletes from that group of 37 pieces those which have variants of the "Komaru" backstamp. (If you have never heard of this term, do not be alarmed. I have picked this mark because many experienced collectors would describe it as "fairly well known." It was used on pieces meant for export to Great Britain. The "Komaru" backstamp will be explained, shown, and discussed later.) When these pieces are eliminated from the total, there are only four pieces left. This number is less than 0.3 of 1%!

In other words, if one were to trouble themselves to learn just *two general types* of backstamps, it can be expected that *more than 99%* of the pieces shown in the Van Patten books will have one of them. Even if all the *specific* kinds of stamps enumerated by Van Patten are counted, only 15 of the 99 numbered backstamps actually occur on any of the non-dinnerware pieces shown in these books. Ten of these are a version of the number "27" backstamp and two are versions of the "Komaru" stamp. This leaves just three other backstamps which appear *on a grand total of only 4 pieces.*

Although some people may actually have memorized the numbers and associated details of those 15 backstamps, I doubt that many have. I certainly have not, and I spend a great deal of time with Noritake backstamps. Please do not misunderstand me; I am *not* suggesting that the details about those 15 backstamps or any others are unimportant or uninteresting. Nor am I suggesting that the other backstamps don't exist, although some may have been included erroneously. Many of those other 48 backstamps, for example, are found on dinnerware items which Van patten shows elsewhere in her book but which are excluded from this book.

I also am not suggesting that knowledge of backstamps or numerical assignment of backstamps is a complete waste of time. I and other serious collectors and dealers in Noritake porcelains are forever indebted not only to Joan Van Patten but also to Lou Ann Donahue, Aimee Neff Alden, Marian Kinney Richardson, and others for their efforts to describe, date, and otherwise discuss Noritake backstamps. Because of their tireless work, it is now unnecessary to seek information about the dates of registration or initial use of backstamps cataloged by these pioneering authors. More importantly, because of the work of these authors, it is finally possible to develop a new *structured* backstamp numbering system which is more informative and easier to use. Without the hard work of the aforementioned people, this task would have been impossible. Although the rationale for this system is discussed below (pp. 30-34), there are several issues that must first be addressed.

What are the most important Noritake backstamps?

Years ago, contestants on the program "Name That Tune" competed with each other to name a tune after hearing the fewest notes. I mention this because, in a sense, I approached the subject of Noritake backstamps with a similar outlook. My goal was to see how small a number I could get by with. I did this because I wanted to make it as easy as possible to learn what was necessary to be reasonably effective as a collector or dealer.

Of course, the key here is what is meant by the phrase "reasonably effective." Ironically, the phrase can have valid meanings that would enable one to establish that *zero* was the smallest number possible. Think about it. Most collectors are not collecting backstamps. Instead, they are collecting beautiful designs and motifs and/or fascinating shapes. From that perspective, it does (or should) not matter what the backstamp is. That said, one could simply decide to skip the entire subject!

If one agrees, however, that some knowledge of backstamps is useful–e.g., if it is suggested that, if nothing else, a limited knowledge of backstamps helps to understand the conversation of other collectors and dealers–then the smallest number

of *general types* of "Noritake" backstamps that one must recognize to be an effective collector or dealer is *three.* Ordered by 1) "importance" in the eyes of collectors and dealers who are likely to use this book and 2) "commonality" as measured by what appears most often on the pieces shown in this book, the three are: 1) "M-in-Wreath;" 2) "Cherry Blossom;" and 3) "Komaru." In this chapter, as in the entire book, the emphasis is on these three stamps. If one wishes to extend this list, three additional general types may be worth mention, although they are *far* less important: 4) "Bowl-in-Wreath;" 5) "N-in-Wreath;" and 6) "Komaru-in-Wreath."

3.1 M-in-Wreath backstamp.

3.2 Cherry Blossom backstamp.

3.3 Komaru backstamp.

3.4 Bowl-in-Wreath backstamp.

3.5 N-in-Wreath backstamp.

3.6 Komaru-in-Wreath backstamp.

Is the "Cherry Blossom" mark a Noritake backstamp?

The Noritake Company itself has little information available on the variety of backstamps which have been used over the years. The information that the company does provide neither mentions nor shows the "Cherry Blossom" backstamp. Because of this and other factors, many have doubted whether pieces with variations of this backstamp were "Noritake" pieces.

In this book, pieces with this backstamp have been included as "Noritake" wares. I suspect for some collectors and dealers, this decision may not "ring true" until more definitive information becomes available from the company itself. I, too, would like such information, but I hope readers with this opinion will consider two other kinds of evidence which I present here.

One key source of information about the status of this backstamp is the previously published views of experts. One such expert was the late Dr. Howard Kottler, a noted ceramist and a colleague of mine at the University of Washington. (A beautifully illustrated and interesting biography of Professor Kottler has been written by Patricia Failing and published by The University of Washington Press; see bibliography.)

Howard Kottler was both an early and enthusiastic collector of Noritake porcelains made during the 1920s. In 1982, an exhibit of a portion of his marvelous collection was organized by Washington State University and the Smithsonian Institution Traveling Exhibition Service. Accompanying this eye-popping exhibit was a "catalog" entitled *Noritake Art Deco Porcelains: Collection of Howard Kottler*. This important but now out-of-print work consists of some excellent color photographs, a list of the pieces in the exhibit (including dimensions and backstamp information), and several brief essays by various experts on a variety of subjects pertinent to the displayed materials (see bibliography).

Some of the materials in the catalog pertained to the production of the Noritake wares Kottler collected, with a passion few others could hope (or want) to match. These materials were partly derived from interviews conducted in Japan with elderly persons who were among the artisans who produced these wares. Based on those interviews and other materials, Dr. Kottler states quite plainly (p. 57) that the "Cherry Blossom" backstamp was "registered in 1924" and that it was "the second most frequently used backstamp for wares directly imported into the United States," presumably during the period of greatest interest to him, which is 1921 through 1941. He also notes (p. 58) that there is no documented explanation for the meaning (if any) of the colors of the backstamp (green, red, and blue).

Since the Noritake Company has not published information which authenticates this backstamp, and since Dr. Kottler does not state explicitly that this backstamp was registered *by* the Noritake Company (although this clearly seems implicit from the context), more than a few collectors and dealers have lingering doubts about its authenticity, even after the catalog on the Kottler collection became available. Thus, it was of great interest 5 years later (in 1987), when Aimee Neff Alden and Marian Kinney Richardson published their book, *Early Noritake China: An Identification and Value Guide to Tableware Patterns*. In this book, the authors provide useful additional information on the "Cherry Blossom" backstamp, although their views are not entirely independent of Dr. Kottler's (e.g., the authors list the Kottler catalog in their bibliography, Dr. Kottler is mentioned in the book's "Acknowledgments," and the authors include some beautiful color photos of some of Kottler's "salesman's book" pages of Noritake dinnerware patterns).

Specifically, Alden and Richardson suggest on page 21 of their book, that what they identify as backstamp MM-17 is a "forerunner of the well-known 'Cherry Blossom' backstamp." They also note that the cherry blossom motif itself is part of a backstamp (MM-23) used on dinnerware in the Elmonte pattern. They show a variation of the MM-17 stamp, cataloged in their book as backstamp MM-17A, which includes the word "Noritake." This fact leads them to conclude that the "Cherry Blossom" backstamp is, thereby, "legitimatized" [sic]. In my opinion, all of this information is certainly reasonable and may even be "true." Even so, people remain skeptical, since the "Cherry Blossom" element of their backstamp MM-17 is similar to, but not the *same* as, the true "Cherry Blossom" backstamps (e.g., MM-23). Given this fact, I turn to a second, more physical, piece of evidence.

3.7 Bowl with double backstamp.

3.8 Back of bowl showing double backstamp.

Photo 3.7 shows a pleasing but otherwise fairly ordinary bowl with a strong floral motif, not unlike Noritake pieces produced and exported in the 1920s. The blank is very similar to others known, by virtue of the backstamp, to have been produced and decorated by the Noritake Company. Several of these are shown in Chapter B (photos B.98, B.100, and B.101). As it happens, all of those pieces have variations of backstamp 27. Therefore, the bowl shown here may be thought of: 1) as somewhat unusual because it is marked with a "Komaru" backstamp (in green) and 2) as being *extremely* unusual because it also has (see photo 3.8) a "Cherry Blossom" backstamp (in red).

Ordinarily, when backstamps are found on items with a glazed bottom, such as this piece, they cannot be felt with the fingertips. (When a backstamp is on an *unglazed* surface, it also is impossible to detect the backstamp by touching it; this is because it is all but impossible to distinguish by touch alone the texture of the clay from the subtle texture of a backstamp.) The subtle texture of the red "Cherry Blossom" backstamp on *this* piece, however, can easily be felt and shows beyond any doubt that this backstamp is *not under* the glaze. On the other hand, the "Komaru" backstamp on this piece does seem to be under the glaze. When touched, the general but minimally rough texture of the sort felt when touching the "Cherry Blossom" backstamp is simply not there. The difference is quite pronounced and can be felt by anyone. Strangely enough, there are nearly a dozen small indentations on the "Komaru" backstamp on this piece; each one *exactly* on the green lines of the backstamp. I have never felt such indentations on any other backstamp, although I certainly have not felt them all.

It is difficult to say why both marks are on one piece. Apparently, at the time the "Komaru" backstamp was applied, something was pressed firmly against the clay, leaving the nearly pinhead-sized marks I describe, as if a hard, perhaps imperfect metal die was used. After the piece was glazed and fired, the second mark was added–but by whom and why? A partial answer may come from Dr. Kottler's previously noted quotation– namely, "Cherry Blossom" pieces were intended for export to the United States. Pieces with a "Komaru" backstamp were intended for export to England (or other parts of the British Commonwealth). Perhaps, prior to shipment, the destination of this piece was changed. Plausible as this explanation may be, it is not without its difficulties.

On page 57 of the previously mentioned catalog, Dr. Kottler indicates the following about "Cherry Blossom" backstamps: pieces with this mark were decorated by various subcontractors of the Noritake Company, not company artisans. Since there are no reports of "Komaru"-backstamped pieces decorated by non-Noritake subcontractors, the bowl shown above appears to be a true paradox: all pieces bearing a "Komaru" mark appear to have been decorated by Noritake Company artisans, and all pieces bearing the "Cherry Blossom" backstamp apparently were decorated by subcontractors, yet this piece has *both* marks.

There is one other form of physical evidence that must be mentioned, which also cuts both ways. I refer to the character and quality of the blanks and decorations on pieces with "Cherry Blossom" backstamp. Experienced collectors believe, with good reason, that some pieces with such backstamps are slightly different in size and other details from what appear to be their Noritake equivalents. Sometimes, as well, there appear to be no exact Noritake equivalents of some blanks with "Cherry Blossom" backstamps. Also, the quality range of pieces with "Cherry Blossom" backstamps is greater, or believed by many to be, than the quality of pieces marked with clearly-identified Noritake Company backstamps. To some (including Dr. Kottler), this finding is accounted for by the fact that pieces bearing this backstamp were decorated by subcontractors. Indeed, it is such differences in quality that have led other collectors and dealers to continue to suggest that the "Cherry Blossom" mark is not a Noritake Company backstamp, and therefore, that such a mark does not identify a "Noritake collectible."

This view is undermined by the fact that there are some cases when it is simply impossible, by examining blanks and/or decorations with the unaided eye, to distinguish "Cherry Blossom"-marked pieces from Noritake-backstamped pieces. In this book, this scenario is best illustrated by two vases shown in photo V.26 (see p. 259). Of course, as readers, you have only a

photo to rely upon, and this is not enough. Short of readers actually seeing the pieces someday (they are owned by a collector in Seattle), I am able only to offer this information: so far, *none* of the scores of experienced Noritake collectors and dealers who have seen these vases could find a difference between the two, even though the backstamps differ. Also, *no one* could point to a feature of either that could lead to a reliable identification of which vase carried which mark.

In summary, the evidence can be thought of as somewhat mixed. In light of this, collectors and dealers may insist that the prudent step is to hold firm until a definitive answer is provided by the Noritake Company. I understand this point of view, and I certainly would welcome any information that would settle the matter one way or the other. In the meantime, I have made a different choice. I am persuaded by the evidence given above that "Cherry Blossom"-backstamped pieces represent a legitimate segment of "Noritake collectibles." In other words, I am persuaded that the link between pieces with "Cherry Blossom" backstamps and the Noritake Company is *quite close indeed,* and therefore, pieces bearing this mark certainly warrant a showing in this book.

What is a "Komaru" Backstamp?

The "Komaru" backstamp (see p. 27) is one of the most important general types of backstamps found on Noritake collectibles. In the following paragraphs, I discuss features of these backstamps that the collector may wish to note from time to time. Before turning to those features, I'd like to comment on one of the names for this backstamp group. Many collectors, apparently based on Donahue's comments (p.69 of her book), refer to pieces with backstamps of this sort as pieces with a "spider" marking. This name is derived from the central element of the backstamp, although the element has only six "legs" rather than eight.

I comment on this usage for three reasons. First, this name nicely illustrates a point that I believe to be true and reasonable about Noritake collectors. It shows that, for the most part, it does not matter to most which specific number a backstamp might have in catalog lists of them. All that is needed, most of the time, is a *general* sense of what the backstamp is. Thus, the collector who knows that one name for a backstamp, such as the above, is "spider," usually will have learned what they want to know when they are told that a piece has "some type of 'spider' backstamp" (collectors make general comments of this sort all the time). Using a name for a general kind of backstamp is an easy and effective way to communicate general information. I note this here because I believe collectors should be encouraged to continue this *general* habit.

Second, this habit shows that Noritake collectors find it convenient to refer to a backstamp by what is thought of as a "name." Although numbers under the right circumstances often become "names" (i.e., something more than "mere" numbers), it would seem prudent to use names without number terms if this is feasible. I make this point because by doing so, I hope to encourage collectors and dealers to continue using non-numerical names for backstamps they frequently encounter, rather than trying to learn which number a backstamp may be cataloged under (*regardless* of the numbering system used).

Third (and on the other side of the ledger), I want to note that "spider" is not the most appropriate name for this type of backstamp. Contrary to "common knowledge" among some collectors and dealers, the central element of this backstamp has nothing to do with the Japanese or Chinese character meaning "spider." Rather, that "six-legged" element with the circle around it is *derived from* a character meaning "difficult." If another character is placed next to that character, it becomes *komaru*: "difficulty." Hence, "Komaru" is the most appropriate name for this backstamp.

One might ask why a version of the character for "difficult" would be part of an entire class of Noritake backstamps? The Noritake Company provides part of the answer in a small pamphlet. The founders of the Noritake Company, establishing a commercial enterprise in the United States when they did, expected to encounter difficulties. As stated in the pamphlet:

> In the export business we had to deal with people . . . who thought and acted in a manner somewhat different from [what] we were accustomed to. Since we had to overcome these difficulties, we chose this character and drew a new design. This progressive thinking is [characteristic] of the people of the Meiji Era.

Keep in mind, however, that the "Komaru" element of the Noritake backstamp would not normally be seen to mean "difficult" by anyone who reads Japanese. That is, if you point out this backstamp to a person who reads Japanese, it is very unlikely that the person will look at it and say, "Ah, that means 'difficult.'" This is because the character has been redrawn, as was noted in the material quoted above. It was redrawn in two ways and it is interesting to note how and why the company produced this "new design" or how and why they modified the character for "difficult."

The square that comprises part of the character for "difficult" has been changed to a circle. Why? So far as I know, the Noritake Company has provided no answer to this question. The change is consistent, however, with an aspect of the Japanese view of squares versus circles and, by extension, an aspect of the Japanese view of how people should relate to each other and the world. There is a saying, in Japanese–*"Kado ga tatsu"*–meaning, essentially "corners stand out" and thereby bring on difficulties. Knowing this, the change from a square to a circle becomes easier to understand. On a circle, there are no corners that stand out and by comparison with a square, a circle will pass smoothly through the situations it gets into.

Also, the shape of the element was altered within the circle. Normally, the top two "arms" of the upper half of this element (other than the vertical "arm" in the middle) are *horizontal* in orientation. In the backstamp, these parts have been shifted upward significantly. Again, although the Noritake Company has not commented about this, the resulting shape does suggest a spear point seen in cross section or "head on." In Japan, a spear is a Shinto good luck symbol; spears, or their symbolic counterparts, are used to "break bad luck."

To summarize, rather than "spoke," "tree," "wheel," or "spider" (all of which are terms that have been used for this backstamp), there are reasons for believing that the central element in question may well be a spear. Even so, the most appropriate name for backstamps with this element would be "Komaru," because this word is most closely linked to the principal idea behind the design.

Cataloging Backstamps: Names, Numbers, and Systems

Previously, I argued for the use of "names" as designations for "general types" of backstamps and, prior to that, I also identified the six most important ones. In creating captions for the photographs in this book, I wanted (and presumed that most readers would as well) to identify backstamps more precisely than simply noting the type found on a piece. To satisfy this need and my own desire for a simpler backstamp cataloging system, I found that I had to develop a new method for numbering backstamps.

I describe this new method in the next few pages. Although reading this section can be helpful, it is not essential to do so in order to use the new system. For those who do not want to learn about the details of the rationale for the system, there is a summary in the Introduction to Part Two of this book (pp. 42-43). Alternatively, some readers may prefer to skip ahead to the pages in this chapter where there are color photographs of backstamps found on pieces shown in this book, along with their identification numbers and other information (pp. 35-41).

For those who do want to know what I did and why, I begin by noting the four goals I set out to achieve and which I used to evaluate preliminary versions of the system.

First, the system must be simple and easy to use. This was one of my most basic goals. I did not want a complicated system, and I presumed the reader did not want that, either. I put considerable effort into developing a system that, in terms of *use*, is simple, simple, simple. For me, simplicity of use meant two things, primarily: 1) the reader should have to know only a few basic things to use the system; and 2) the reader should, with the backstamp number alone, have a good idea of what the *basic* characteristics of the backstamp are without having to know a lot of arcane, arbitrary, hard-to-remember facts.

Second, the system must be flexible. For me, achieving this goal primarily has meant that when new backstamps are discovered, it should be possible to assign a number to them quickly, easily, and in a way that does not undermine the gains made through the features of the carefully developed new system.

Third, if possible, the system should give some clues about chronology. For me, this was the least important of the goals. When I set out to create the system, I believed that if the general backstamp numbers could indicate approximate chronology, this would be a worthwhile "bonus." As it turned out, the best I could do was to get the new backstamp numbers to convey chronology *roughly*.

Fourth, the system must look familiar, especially to experienced Noritake collectors and dealers. In some respects, this goal was one of the most important. Specifically, my aim was to overcome the few key problems inherent in Van Patten's method, by developing a new system that would at least *resemble* Van Patten's even if mine was quite different, as I was almost sure it would be. I believed it was essential to achieve this goal for one simple reason: there is no way to expect people to adopt a system of numbering that *looks* totally different from one they currently use and have known for years.

A taxonomy of Noritake backstamps.

There is a close connection between my previous discussion of what the smallest number of backstamp types might be and the way I have assigned numbers both to the Noritake backstamps that appear on pieces in this book and others that are known but not represented here. What I have attempted to develop *approximates* a taxonomic system–that is, a system for organizing backstamps that is *approximately* similar to the system used by biologists to group animals.

Biologists do not simply assign "catalog numbers" successively to living things as they are discovered until they all have been numbered. Such a system would quickly become too large and disorganized to be efficient. Instead, biologists have created taxonomies of living things. Taxonomies are groups arranged hierarchically by a process of inclusion, based on features at each level that are both important and distinctive (e.g., whether an animal eats meat or grass). Then, instead of having to learn the names and features of thousands of animals and plants, biologists and most of the rest of us get along simply by using the more general information associated with various "types" or classes of animals.

Accordingly, I set out to give a kind of taxonomic structure to the list of known Noritake backstamps. It quickly became apparent, however, that the facts about Noritake backstamps and the four goals I had established for a new system would force me to choose between a system with dozens of fairly homogeneous types or one with a smaller number of less homogeneous types. I chose the latter option. Once this was decided, I found there were other problems to solve. Consequently, I tried *many* versions before settling upon the backstamp numbering system used in this book.

There are basically three levels in this taxonomic system (it can be expanded in the future if necessary—one reason for the taxonomic approach). From most general or inclusive to least, these levels are: 1) general types; 2) specific kinds; and 3) varieties. Below is a list of the *general types* of backstamps found on Noritake collectibles (excluding dinnerware for the most part).

0_. Early, infrequently seen backstamps
1_. Early "Komaru" and "Cherry Blossom" backstamps
2_. "M-in-Wreath" backstamps (#27 and others from the 1920s)
3_. "Post-M-in-Wreath" backstamps, including "M-with-Banner-and-Crown"
4_. "M-in-Wreath-with-Bow" and related backstamps (none in this book)
5_. Later "Komaru," "Komaru-in-Wreath" and other post-1940 backstamps
6_. "Bowl-in-Wreath" and other pre-"N-in-Wreath" backstamps
7_. "N-in-Wreath" and "Noritake Bone China" backstamps
8_. Contemporary "Brand name" backstamps
9_. Highly specialized, limited-use backstamps (none in this book)

Most readers may wonder why there are lines after the numbers, and some may be surprised to see that the list begins with zero; of course, there are reasons for this. To explain my reasoning, I must indicate how the backstamp numbers used in this book are structured or, more importantly, what they mean. In terms of structure, the numbers consist of two digits to the left of a decimal and from one to three digits to the right of it. In general form, the vast majority of the numbers will look like this: ##.#, while some will look like this: ##.##, or even this: ##.###. In this system, information is conveyed *both* by the numerals themselves *and* by their location in the different parts of the number. For example, the numeral located two places to the *left* of the decimal designates the ten *general types* of backstamp found on "Noritake collectibles." It is these numerals which are given in the list above.

A numeral will be placed in the space immediately to the left of the decimal (this place is indicated in the list by the short line). The numeral in that spot designates a *specific kind* of each of the ten general types of backstamps listed above. The details of the rationale used to assign the numerals in the unit's place will not be discussed here, except to say that they were assigned in as orderly a fashion as possible, given the four goals for the system (particularly the fourth goal—produce a new system that looked familiar to other well-known ones). Below, additional details on this process for the important "20s" group of backstamps will be presented.

The numerals to the right of the decimal denote the colors of the backstamp and, thereby, designate *varieties* of the specific kind of backstamp. For example, most collectors and dealers know that the famous number "27" backstamp comes in green or red (also called maroon by some collectors and dealers). This backstamp comes in other colors as well, but this is less widely known and is unimportant here. To designate varieties in terms of backstamp colors, the number to the right of the decimal is established using the list below.

.0 = green
.1 = red (or maroon)
.2 = blue
.3 = magenta (similar to but not the same as red)
.4 = teal (similar to but not the same as blue)
.5 = black
.6 = yellow (including mustard and other similar shades but not gold)
.7 = gold
.8 = "silver" (including metallic, which is rare; found when a backstamp is embossed in metal)
.9 = tan, brown, beige, and other similar shades

Collectors and dealers who are convinced that backstamp color is of importance may wish to memorize the first three colors in this list, because they are *by far* the most common colors of the backstamps on the pieces shown in this book.

Normally, Noritake backstamps on pieces prior to about 1940 had only one color, and the numbers for the backstamps typically found on these pieces will be of the ##.# form (e.g., 27.1). A few, however, have two colors (usually in the form of a backstamp with two distinct parts, often separated by quite some distance). These can and will be identified by a backstamp number of this form: ##.## (two numbers to the right of the decimal indicating the two colors in the backstamp). For example, suppose a backstamp has two colors: green and red. Such a backstamp would have a number like this: ##.01. The order of these numbers does not signify anything of substance (for example, it does *not* indicate what the predominant color is). Rather, they are simply given in numerical order (from low to high, left to right). For many of the backstamps commonly in use after about 1940, it is not unusual to see three colors. A backstamp that has green, red, and brown (or beige or tan), for example, would be ##.019.

But, because all 10 digits have already been used and because it cannot be presumed that all Noritake backstamps are known, what numeral would be assigned if a backstamp should be found with a color not listed above? This is a very good question, and in answering it, it will be possible to illustrate the flexibility of this taxonomic numbering system. Letters and/or other numerals can be added to the basic string of numerals which serve as the building blocks of the backstamp numbers used in this book. These new components would be used to handle details about backstamps which are presently unknown or if known, are not encoded (e.g., because they are believed to be unimportant). When necessary, the numerals can be distinguished from the core or basic backstamp numbers by using a slash (/).

For example, if a backstamp is found with orange as one of its colors, it could be designated as follows: ##.#/1 (with the 1 after the slash designating orange; this would, of course, have to be noted clearly in material published about the revised system). If orange happened to be the *only* color, the backstamp would be ##./1 (the space after the decimal is empty, because it is reserved for designating colors listed above, in which orange is not included).

Not all additional information must be handled in this way. For example, information about "design" numbers and pattern names are not encoded with numerals in the backstamp number. Instead, in this book, they are recorded within parentheses immediately after the backstamp number. For example, the word

"Roseara" will be found within parentheses after the backstamp number. Similarly, design numbers such as the commonly seen "19322" (the number on Azalea pieces) and "25920" are written within parentheses after the backstamp number. There is not much known about the significance, if any, of these numbers, although some collectors have speculated that the first two digits on the left may be the year when the piece was produced.

It would have been possible, with a taxonomic numbering system, to use a numerical code for pattern names and design numbers. Indeed, several preliminary systems were developed to do this. However, these methods were extremely complex and would have been difficult to use. There simply would have been too many specific kinds and varieties of backstamps. Besides, it just seemed silly to use a numeral in a certain position in the backstamp number to encode a number, especially when: 1) there already are quite a few such numbers; and 2) more numbers could be discovered in the future. Instead, I decided simply to supply the pattern or design numbers within the caption. This is much easier than forcing users to choose between either looking up a backstamp number to find out what the design number is or, worse yet, having to memorize such a complex system. Similarly, I also provide the pattern names in the captions because Roseara and Azalea are the only two distinctively backstamped dinnerware patterns included within this book.

In this book, there are a number of pieces which have backstamps consisting only of the words "Made in Japan" or "Japan." Pieces with such backstamps are parts of what at one time were larger, multipiece sets which would have had at least one piece with the full backstamp. Usually these "Made in Japan"- or "Japan"-marked pieces are too small to have a full backstamp. In a few cases, the pieces are large enough, but apparently for reasons of economy, the Noritake Company chose not to provide full backstamps on all the pieces in a set. In this book, these backstamps are designated as follows (with the color indicated by the numeral after the decimal):

> MIJ.# = Made in Japan
> J.# = Japan

Because many non-Noritake Company Japanese ceramic items have backstamps with the words "Made in Japan" or "Japan," collectors and dealers should keep in mind that Noritake items with only these words as backstamp were part of sets with a full backstamp. Thus, the colors, letter shape, and other details of Noritake MIJ.# or J.# backstamps should be examined carefully, as Kottler notes on p. 58 of *Noritake Art Deco Porcelains*. So far, the only known Noritake MIJ.# or J.# backstamps are green and red. All of the MIJ.# or J.# backstamps in this book are on pieces which appear to have been parts of sets with variations of backstamp number "27."

In this context, we also may note how the taxonomic numbering system in this book conveys a *rough* estimate of various chronological matters–an interest that often initially motivates people to search for information about backstamps. One can gain a sense of chronology in two ways. First, the larger the number two places to the left of the decimal, the newer the mark is. Second, that numeral often designates the *approximate decade* of this century during which the backstamp was either introduced or in widest use. This is most evident for the all-important "20s" group of backstamps. While we are on this subject, in my opinion, collectors and dealers will be no worse and perhaps better off if they attempt to date pieces by using the clues provided by the *motifs on and the style of* pieces rather than those provided by backstamp catalogs which include registration dates and the like. These registration dates often

antedate their use by several years and only a few have a terminal date. For these reasons and others, I recommend directing attention to the side of the piece *opposite* the one with the backstamp.

An Example

To better understand this system, let us begin by considering the "Komaru" backstamp discussed previously. I begin with this backstamp because important features of the general system can be illustrated with this example. In the Van Patten book, there are nine backstamps with variations of the basic "Komaru" marks (i.e., excluding what I refer to above as "Komaru-in-Wreath" backstamps). Three of these (JVP numbers 12, 13, and 14) are Nippon backstamps and are not dealt with further here (I have rules for assigning them taxonomic numbers in my system, but I do not discuss this here). The other five basic "Komaru" backstamps in Van Patten's list are numbers 11, 16, 17, 18, 20, and 90. These numbers, like all the others in the Van Patten catalog, simply locate a backstamp within a non-hierarchical series. Of these, by far the most commonly seen is JVP backstamp number "16."

In the system used in this book, this same "Komaru" backstamp also has been assigned the number "16." The grounds for doing so are different, however. Here, the numeral 1, two places to the left of the decimal, designates the *general type* and the number 6, one place to the left of the decimal, designates the *specific kind* of the general type. In addition, whenever this backstamp is listed (e.g., in a caption in Part Two) there also will be various numerals to the right of the decimal (e.g., it could be, depending upon the circumstances, 16.0, 16.1, or 16.3, among others). The numerals to the right of the decimal indicate the color(s) of the backstamp. Thus, with this system, it is not necessary to indicate the variety by writing things like "red number 16" or "backstamp number 16 in red." Instead, all of this can be conveyed simply by writing "16.1." This efficiency is one of the benefits of this system.

The other known "Komaru" backstamps (except for JVP #90) have been or will be assigned other numbers from 10 through 15 using the numbering system in this book. Because not all of these backstamps occur on pieces shown in this book, they are not all listed in the table at the end of this chapter. Even so, in this book, whenever you see a backstamp with a number from 10 through 16, you can be sure that it has the "Komaru" symbol without a wreath as well as various words (e.g, "Noritake" or "Made in Japan"). If details are to be known, they must be looked up in Table 3.1–a step even more necessary with other backstamp-numbering systems. If this sounds demanding, remember the previous discussion regarding how few of the 100-plus known backstamps actually appear on the (non-dinnerware) pieces shown in this or similar books. Only a few numbers will occur with any frequency and be worth committing to memory.

These points apply for the numbers designating colors, as well. Although I did not report this previously when discussing the data on backstamps of the pieces shown in the two Van Patten volumes, it turns out that 94% of those pieces have a number "27" backstamp in red or green (the percent would be higher if full information were available on the 12 pieces listed as "27" without a color designation). This means that if: 1) you are interested in pieces of the sort shown in the Van Patten books and this book; and 2) you are interested in knowing the color of the backstamp listed for a piece, you can be on top of the matter nearly 90% of the time simply by remembering that, in the system employed in this book, a ".0" designates green and a ".1" designates red.

As an aside to those who may wonder why I did not use mnemonic letters such as "G" or "R" instead of numerals ".0" and ".1," the reason may be discovered by answering two questions: 1) what letter would be used for gold coloring; and 2) would the letter "B" designate blue, black, or brown?

Not all known distinctive features of the "Komaru" backstamps are encoded by the system used here (or by the others published elsewhere). For example, the "spear" element in the center of the circle varies in numerous ways which are hard to describe and few collectors notice. Sometimes the points are sharp, sometimes they are comparatively broad or fat-looking, sometimes they are thin or dull. Other features also vary in small, easily overlooked ways. Sometimes there is an accent mark over the "e" in "Noritake," and sometimes there is not. Also, there are differences in the shades of blue in this backstamp and there are differences in the shape of the cursive letter "r" in Noritake; sometimes the "r" is "flat-topped," and sometimes it is not.

Although some differences may be encoded by the way in which they correlate with encoded features such as color (e.g., all the backstamps with the flat-topped "r" that I have seen are teal colored), I have not systematically, numerically encoded the features mentioned in the previous paragraph. This is because there is little or no available information regarding how such variations pertain to such issues as chronology or to the country to which these pieces were shipped. Moreover, few if any collectors consistently note these features when discussing this backstamp, and none have informed me of these details regarding the "Komaru" backstamps on their pieces. Consequently, variations in shape of the "spear," the shape of the "r," and accent marks are ignored in the backstamp catalog I have developed for this book.

Another point may be discussed here regarding the numbers for the "Komaru" general type of backstamp. As you may recall, I noted that the facts about backstamps and the goals I had established for a new system forced me to choose either a system with dozens of homogeneous general types or a system with a small number of less homogeneous general types, and I chose the latter option. Two effects of this decision follow.

First, not all backstamps with the numeral 1, placed two spaces to the left of the decimal, have a "Komaru" symbol. As the name of the "general type" designated by the numeral 1 indicates (it is "Early 'Komaru' and 'Cherry Blossom' backstamps"), some backstamps with the numeral in this place are "Cherry Blossom" backstamps. Specifically, in the system used here, backstamps 17, 18, and 19 are "Cherry Blossom" backstamps. Second, one of the "Komaru" backstamps in the 50s group (the "Komaru-in-wreath and other post-1940s backstamps" group) does not have a wreath. Previously, I mentioned this backstamp (JVP #90) and indicated more would be said about it. This backstamp has the "Komaru" symbol but does not have a wreath. It was assigned a 50s number because it is known to have been registered in 1949. Here, I was faced with assigning a number based on appearance or on registration date; I chose the latter. In other words, this system is not "perfect."

Numbering the "M-in-Wreath" Backstamps

As you may have noticed already, the *vast* majority of the pieces depicted here have a backstamp with a number in the 20s (e.g., 27.0, 28.1, 29.1). Because these are so numerous, the principles used when assigning numbers to backstamps are discussed here in detail. In an effort to simplify this discussion, an "outline" format is used. The reader need not "study" this material; it is here primarily to provide details that may be used later to answer questions about the relationship between the number of a backstamp and its features.

After this material is presented, it is summarized in three "basic principles." If you become familiar with these three principles, you will seldom need to consult this chapter to understand the captions. Those people already familiar with the Van Patten backstamp-numbering system should find the principles easy to assimilate and could even skip the outline and go directly to the "basic principles" (p. 34).

In outline form, here are the four basic rules that were used to assign "20s" numbers to Noritake backstamps.

1. To be assigned a number in the 20s, a Noritake backstamp *must* have a capital letter "M" within a laurel or other "wreath" (hence the name for the *general type*: "M-in-Wreath").

2. In addition to the word "Noritake," (found on nearly all the backstamps in this book and on all but one backstamp of this general type), the following words known to appear in various combinations on these backstamps will affect the numeral one place to the *left* of the decimal, which designates a *specific kind* of "20s" backstamp:
   a. Japan
   b. Made in
   c. Handpainted
   d. Design Pat[ent] Applied For
   e. Chinese/Japanese characters (which, in all the cases known so far, are merely the Japanese version of item d, above).

3. For the backstamps in the "20s" group, the following characteristics have *no impact* on the assignment of a backstamp numeral (the numeral one to the left of the decimal point) designating a *specific kind* of "20s" backstamp:
   a. the overall size of the backstamp
   b. variations from one stamp to the next in the size of the letters
   c. small variations from one backstamp to the next in color saturation and/or shading
   d. post-production alterations of the backstamp (e.g., those brought about by the use of abrasives to remove the word "Japan")
   e. the presence of numerals (design numbers) and/or the word "No." [number]
   f. the presence of the abbreviations U.S. [United States] or J. [Japan] or of the word "Japanese"
   g. the presence or content of pattern names

Note: As noted above, design numbers and pattern names will be noted within parentheses after the backstamp number—for example, 28.1(Roseara) or 29.1(25920).

4. The following feature of Noritake backstamps has a bearing on the numeral assigned to the *right* of the decimal in the "20s" group:
   a. color (the specific effect of this factor on the numeral was discussed previously).

The backstamp numbers to the left of the decimal for the 20s "M-in-Wreath" group of backstamps are defined as follows:

   20. = this number is not currently assigned to any backstamp
   21. = a large "M" inside an abstract wreath with the word "Japan" beneath; no "Noritake"
   22. = this number is not currently assigned to any backstamp
   23. = this number is not currently assigned to any backstamp

24. = M-in-Wreath plus the word "Japan" (no "Made in") below the wreath

25. = M-in-Wreath plus "Handpainted" and "Japan" below the wreath

26. = M-in-Wreath plus the words "Made in Japan" (but no "Handpainted")

27. = M-in-Wreath plus "Handpainted" and "Made in Japan" below the wreath

28. = M-in-Wreath plus the words "Design Patent Applied For"–no matter what other words or symbols there may be. That is, this designation is not affected by variations created by the presence of abbreviations/words that modify this basic phrase (e.g., "Pat." instead of "Patent;" a country designation such as "Japanese" or "U.S." or "J;") nor does it matter if elsewhere in the backstamp a pattern name appears; if it says "Made in Japan" or just "Japan;" if the word "Handpainted" is a part of this backstamp or not.

29. = M-in-Wreath plus the presence of any Chinese/Japanese characters–no matter what other words or symbols there may be. That is, this designation is not affected by variations created by the presence of Chinese characters that vary in meaning; similarly, it does not matter if elsewhere in the backstamp a pattern name appears; if it says "Made in Japan" or just "Japan;" or if the word "Handpainted" is a part of this backstamp or not.

As noted previously, color modifies the decimal number of the backstamp. This has the effect of conveying quickly and easily the color(s) of any backstamp in the "20s" group. The most common colors are green (.0) and red (.1); magenta (.3) is sometimes seen and blue (.2) is known, although apparently rare. One case of a silver (metallic) (.8) "M-in-Wreath" backstamp is known, although it is not shown in this book.

The experienced collector or dealer reading this may have noticed that certain details of the "M-in-Wreath" backstamps are ignored (this also is true of the "Komaru," "Cherry Blossom," and other backstamps). "What!?!," I hear some of you saying, "How can he do that?" In a sense, it is easy, because I mean that I have ignored certain details when assigning a backstamp number. For example, as noted above, some "M-in-Wreath" backstamps include what seems to be a pattern number. I see no need to assign a separate backstamp number for each such example. For readers who object on the grounds that valuable information may be lost, let me hasten to add that this information *is* included in the photo captions, at least when the information was initially available.

Thus, in Part Two of this book, a caption may be found with the backstamp entry written like this: 29.1 (25920). After a little experience with this system, the reader will *at a glance* know from the .1 that the backstamp is red (or maroon), and from the 2, that it is an "M-in-Wreath" backstamp. From the 9, it can be determined that it is a *specific kind* of the "M-in-Wreath" general type; however, if you are like me, you may not be certain *from memory* what that means, and you will need to look it up if you really care. When you do look it up, you will see that the 9 designates "M-in-Wreath" backstamps with Chinese/Japanese characters in them. The number in parentheses after the backstamp number is the design number shown as part of the backstamp.

Evaluating the system

Is this system actually simpler? You bet it is. Consider this one example: more than half a dozen distinct backstamp numbers are needed in the Van Patten system to identify the presence of a Chinese/Japanese character meaning "number" or an English abbreviation for the same idea ("No."). Although such information may *potentially* be of general interest someday, these are details which, quite frankly, are of no consequence to the typical collector or dealer.

Saying this does introduce a very interesting and important subject. How do we know when a difference matters? The short answer is we don't always know, and when we think we do, we may be wrong. For example, someday it could be shown that there is an important difference (date, quality of porcelain, etc.) between pieces with pattern numbers preceded by the idea of "number" written in Chinese/Japanese characters and pieces with the abbreviation "No." It is a possibility, albeit a remote one. As I have said before, most of us are collecting designs and motifs, not backstamps. Let's keep our priorities straight.

This noted, there still are some interesting issues that must at least be mentioned in this context. For example, what about differences in the color of a backstamp? Many readers of this essay may have wondered if there really is enough difference between "red" and "magenta" to justify assigning different code numbers. It is a good question, and the answer does not contradict the comments made about keeping our priorities straight. Indeed, I chose this issue because it *is* in keeping with those comments.

First, as it happens, there is a difference between the character and (I think) the quality of pieces with magenta "M-in-Wreath" backstamps. Although this may not be recognized unless pieces with red and magenta backstamps are placed side by side, pieces with magenta "M-in-Wreath" backstamps tend to have much finer decorations and more gold than those with red "M-in-Wreath" backstamps. Although this will not prove it, I am quite confident that, without touching a piece, I can pick out the magenta "M-in-Wreath"-backstamped pieces in anybody's collection; they are that different. Second, several later "N-in-Wreath" backstamps are clearly magenta, not red, in color, so the color is needed for these marks. For both reasons, the red-magenta distinction makes a difference and is accordingly encoded in the backstamp-numbering system in this book.

The Three Basic Principles for Mastering "M-in-Wreath" Backstamp Numbers

1. All "M-in-Wreath" backstamps, a general type designated by the numeral 2, two places left of the decimal, have both a laurel or other wreath and a capital "M" inside the wreath (honoring the Morimura brothers who founded the Noritake Company).

2. There are seven specific kinds of "M-in-Wreath" backstamps designated by numerals one place left of the decimal, with the one numbered "7" being the most common. Nearly all of the backstamps within this general type may be thought of as variations of this backstamp. In addition to the word "Noritake" above the wreath, all number "27" backstamps contain the words "Made in Japan" and "Handpainted" below the wreath.

3. For all backstamps in the "20s" group, backstamp color is indicated by the numerals to the right of the decimal. The most commonly seen colors are green (.0), red (.1), blue (.2), and magenta (.3).

Table 3.1: A Master List of the Backstamps Which Appear on the Pieces Shown in this Book

What You Should Know About This Table

This table displays, in summary form, important information about the numbered "specific kinds" of backstamps common to the pieces in this book. The backstamp numbers used in this book are listed in the column headed "DHS #s." Below, more detailed information about these numbers is presented. More of the rationale for the entire backstamp-numbering system was discussed previously in this chapter, although the reader need not review the information to use these numbers. With one or two exceptions, the backstamps described in this table appear on items shown in this book; exceptions are backstamps on pieces which, due mainly to space limitations, do not appear in this book.

This table is *not*, nor was ever intended to be a *complete* compendium of Noritake Company backstamps. As desirable as such a listing might be, its production is for future endeavors. First and foremost, it is not known how many Noritake backstamps there are. Second, I decided long ago that only color photos of backstamps would be shown in this book, even when the backstamp is black and the porcelain background is white. Thus, a few backstamps known and relevant to Noritake collectors are not shown here, either because a photo of the backstamp was unavailable or because a piece bearing the backstamp is not included in Part Two of the book, or both. At least one "variety" of each "specific kind" of Noritake backstamp found on the pieces in Part Two of this book is included here. In some important cases, several varieties are shown.

Third, I also decided long ago that I would not show a backstamp in this book simply because it has the word "Noritake" in it or because some document or previous publication lists a particular array of terms and/or markings as being a "Noritake Company" backstamp. This is not because I believe that some of the backstamps listed in other publications are not really Noritake Company backstamps. Rather, it is because my primary goal here is to provide information about the backstamps which are *relevant* to Noritake collectors and dealers and to leave out ones which are not. Many known Noritake Company backstamps were used on dinnerware items of various kinds which were, after all, the primary porcelain products of the company. Few of these porcelains are of interest to "Noritake collectors," and they are not discussed in this book. Therefore, they are not shown or presented in this table (although the backstamp numbering system used in this book can accommodate these backstamps if need be; this explains some of the "skipped" numbers discussed in the next paragraph).

Although users of this table who have not read the earlier part of this chapter can easily use the information provided here, they may be puzzled to see that some numbers have been skipped (the first backstamp number in the table, for example, is 07.). The unused numbers were not "skipped" accidentally, but rather are simply not currently assigned. This happens because the backstamp-numbering system used here is more than an enumeration of backstamps. In the future, some of the currently unused numbers may be used; some may never be used. The reason for this is discussed in some detail in the chapter text.

Users of this table should also remember that all the backstamp numbers shown in Part Two have numerals to the right of the decimal as well as to the left. Frequently, only the numerals to the left of the decimal are shown here. The numer-

als to the right indicate the colors of the backstamp, and thereby, designate *varieties* of the *specific kinds* of backstamps listed here. Because the vast majority of pieces of interest to Noritake collectors have backstamps in one of three colors (green, red, and blue), one can quickly learn to decode the system for the numerals to the right of the decimal. Information on this may be found on p. 31 of this chapter and in the introduction to Part Two (p. 43).

There are basically two reasons to pay any attention at all to backstamps. For most collectors, the primary issue is about origins: did the Noritake Company actually make the piece I am looking at? The secondary issue is about chronology: when was this piece produced? As it happens, backstamps are more helpful with origins than chronology. Thus, the user of this book who has or is thinking of acquiring a piece which has a backstamp like those shown here can reasonably be sure of two things: 1) that it was made by the Noritake Company; and 2) that it is of interest to (i.e., collected by) many who define themselves as "Noritake collectors." Indeed, even if the piece in question has a backstamp that is only similar to those shown here, the collector may still conclude that it may be a piece made by the Noritake Company. The supposition supporting this would be that the piece happens to have a backstamp that is just a *variation* of one shown here. Because there are backstamps that are similar to ones shown here which either are not or may not be Noritake Company backstamps, however, I advise extreme caution when concluding that such a backstamp *is* a variation of one shown here. In such circumstances, the advice of an expert should be sought.

Matters of chronology are far more problematic than matters of manufacturing. First, information about when the Noritake Company actually used some of their backstamps is simply not available. Second, although previous authors have obtained registration dates for a few backstamps, these dates often provide little more than rough estimates because it is known and/or strongly suspected that some backstamps were used prior to the registration dates and others were not used for some time after they were registered. This situation is compounded by a third issue: some backstamps appear to have been used for a time, then not used, and then changed slightly and used later. If one does not notice such things as small differences in the size and shape of certain letters or the presence or absence of tiny design elements such as dots, one can draw erroneous conclusions about which backstamp is actually used, and thereby, what the age of the piece is. Finally, some backstamps were used for several decades or longer. Given this, collectors and dealers are strongly advised to pay as much attention to matters of decorative style as they do to registration dates of backstamps when attempting to determine the age of a piece of Noritake porcelain.

What the Column Headings Mean

The table below has six columns. Column 1 at the far left (DHS #s) shows, with two exceptions, the numerals designating the "specific kinds" of backstamp relevant to this book. The exceptions are two backstamps designated by letters, either J or MIJ, standing respectively for "Japan" and "Made in Japan." Usually, these words occur on pieces that were parts of larger sets, that were too small to permit the application of the full backstamp, or both. In such cases, the Noritake Company simply marked a piece with the words "Japan" or "Made in Japan." Often, in this column, the numerals shown are only the ones to the left of the decimal; in other cases, however, colors are indicated with the appropriate numerals, and photos of these backstamp varieties are shown. When the color-designating numerals are shown, the backstamp number indicates specific *kind* as well as *variety*.

Column 2 (Description) states, as briefly as possible, what the defining features of the backstamps are. This is a simplified guide only. Users should also consult the photos, and in some cases, rely more upon the photos than the words, because two backstamps with identical words and symbolic elements can be different because of their arrangement. Also in this column,

when appropriate, certain features which one may notice but which are *not* "defining features" will be mentioned. Unless stated otherwise, all of these backstamps contain the word "Noritake" and none have the word "Nippon" except when it is part of the phrase "Nippon Toki Kaisha" which means, in essence, "Japanese Ceramics Company." Column 3 (Year) gives an estimate of the backstamp registration date, from company materials as well as data in the sources shown in columns 4-6. A question mark shows the registration date information is lacking or unconvincing. Columns 4 through 6 (LAD #s, A&R #s, and JVP #s) provide a cross-reference to the backstamp numbers used for these backstamps by respectively, Lou Ann Donahue, Alden and Richardson, and Joan Van Patten.

DHS #s	Defining Features of Specific Types of Noritake Backstamps	Year	LAD#s	A&R#s	JVP#s
J.	The word "Japan" in standard Noritake backstamp red and green colors	1920s mostly	None	None	Non
MIJ.	The words "Made in Japan" in standard Noritake backstamp red and green colors	1920s mostly	None	None	None
07.0	RC + Balance symbol + Nippon Toki Kaisha + Chinese/Japanese characters in green	1906	None	None	7
07.3	RC + Balance symbol + Nippon Toki Kaisha + Chinese/Japanese characters in magenta (found on especially fine, highly decorated sets usually with extensive gold)	1906	None	None	7
07.7	RC + Balance symbol + Nippon Toki Kaisha + Chinese/Japanese characters in gold	1906	None	None	7
14.	Komaru symbol + Made in Japan +Design Patent Applied For (ignores whether there is an accent on the "e" in Noritake as well as the shape of the "r" and the shape of the central element)	?	None	None	17
15.01	Komaru symbol + Made in Japan (in green) + Chinese/Japanese characters (in red) (ignores whether there is a design number, which will be written within parentheses with the backstamp number in the captions), an accent on the "e" in Noritake as well as the shape of the "r" and the shape of the central element)	1908	None	MM-9A	None
16.0	Komaru symbol + Made in Japan in green (but no Chinese/Japanese characters) (ignores whether there is an accent on the "e" in Noritake as well as the shape of the "r" and the shape of the central element)	1908	11	MM-9	16
16.1	Komaru symbol + Made in Japan in red (but no Chinese/Japanese characters) (ignores whether there is an accent on the "e" in Noritake as well as the shape of the "r" and the shape of the central element)	1908	11	MM-9	16
16.4	Komaru symbol + Made in Japan in teal (but no Chinese/Japanese characters) (ignores whether there is an accent on the "e" in Noritake as well as the shape of the "r" and the shape of the central element)	1908	11	MM-9	16
18.	Large letter M inside a thin 5-lobed "cherry blossom" + Made in Japan + the word "Noritake"	c. 1925	None	MM-20	None
19.0	5-lobed "cherry blossom" with a center of radiating lines + Made in Japan or just Japan but without the word "Noritake"; in green; decorated by a subcontractor	1924	None	MM-23 but without a pattern name	None
19.1	5-lobed "cherry blossom" with a center of radiating lines + Made in Japan or just Japan but without the word "Noritake"; in red; decorated by subcontractor	1924	None	MM-23 but without a pattern name	None
19.2	5-lobed "cherry blossom" with a center of radiating lines + Made in Japan or just Japan but without the word "Noritake; in blue; decorated by subcontractor	1924	None	MM-23 but without a pattern name	None
21.	Large letter M inside an abstract wreath + Japan; no "Noritake"	1915-1919	None	MM-15	None
24.	M-in-Wreath + Japan (no "Handpainted" or "Made in")	1918	None	MM-18	52
25.	M-in-Wreath + Handpainted + Japan (no "Made in")	c. 1918	None	MM-26	50
26.0	M-in-Wreath + Made in Japan (no "Handpainted") in green	1921	10	None	38
26.1	M-in-Wreath + Made in Japan (no "Handpainted") in red	1921	10	MM-22	38
27.0	M-in-Wreath + Handpainted + Made in Japan in green	1918	9	MM-19	27
27.1	M-in-Wreath + Handpainted + Made in Japan in red (decorated by Noritake Company subcontractors)	1925	9	MM-19A	27
27.2	M-in-Wreath + Handpainted + Made in Japan in blue (on some items for children)	?	None	None	None
27.3	M-in-Wreath + Handpainted + Made in Japan in magenta (on especially fine, highly decorated sets usually with extensive gold)	?	None	MM-19A	None
28.	M-in-Wreath + Made in Japan + Design Patent Applied For [ignores variations due to abbreviations or whether it has the words "Handpainted" and "Made in"	1921	None	MM-22B & C, + MM-19B	28 + 36, 39, 41-48

DHS #s	Defining Features of Specific Types of Noritake Backstamps	Year	LAD#s	A&R#s	JVP#s
	and/or to the presence of various pattern names, which, in captions, are added in parentheses after the backstamp number–e.g., 28.1 (Roseara)]			& G-L + others	and 98
29.	M-in-Wreath + Made in Japan + any Chinese/Japanese characters [ignores variations due to whether it says "Handpainted" or "Made in" or to the particulars of pattern numbers which, in captions, are added in parentheses after the backstamp number–e.g., 29.1 (29812)–the Azalea pattern number is 19322]	c. 1925	None	MM-19C & D-F	29 + 30-35, 37, 49 & 99
33.	Shield-and-Wreath-under-Crown	?	None	None	None
38.0	M-with-Banner-and-Crown + Handpainted + Japan (in maroon)	1940	None	None? (colors are different)	79
39.	M-with-Banner-and-Crown +Japan (no "Handpainted")	1940	24?	MM-43	None
50.	Komaru symbol + Nippon Toki Kaisha	1949	27	MM-50	90
54.	Komaru-in-Wreath + Made in Japan	?	None	None	None
55.	Komaru-in-Wreath + Bone China + Nippon Toki Kaisha (does not have the word "Noritake")	1940	21	None	80
56.15	Komaru-in-Wreath + Bone China + Nippon Toki Kaisha (in black) + Made in Japan (in red) (does not have the word "Noritake")	1940?	Like 21 but no MIJ	None	Like #80 but no MIJ
64.019	Bowl-in-Wreath + Bone China + Nippon Toki (no "Kaisha"; in green, red & brown)	?	None	None	None
65.019	Bowl-in-Wreath + Bone China + Nippon Toki China + Japan (in green, red and brown)	1949	29	None	85?
65.5	Bowl-in-Wreath + Bone China + Nippon Toki China + Japan (in black)	?	None	None	85
66.57	Bowl-in-Wreath + Bone China + ® +Japan (in black and gold)	?	57	None	86
67.019	Bowl-in-Wreath + Bone China + Nippon Toki Kaisha (no Japan or Made in Japan) (in green, red and brown)	?	None	None	None
70.7	Noritake Bone China Japan in gold (in script; ignores edition numbers and similar details; if information is available will be noted in caption in parentheses after the backstamp number)	?	None	None	None
71.7	Noritake (in script) + (in block letters; in gold) Bone China A Limited Edition (of some number) + Japan	?	None	None	None
72.	N-in-Wreath-with-Bow + Bone China + ® + Japan	?	None	None	None
74.	N-in-Wreath-with-Bow + ® +Japan (ignores variations due to 2 tiny dots in the wreath of some versions)	1964	None	None	94
76.	N-in-Wreath (no bow) + Nippon Toki Kaisha + Japan	post 1953	None	None	96
77.	N-in-Wreath (no bow) + Nippon Toki Kaisha (but no Japan)	post 1953?	None	None	None
78.	N-in-Wreath (no bow) + Studio Collection + Bone China + Japan	?	None	None	None
86.	Noritake Legacy Philippines	?	None	None	None

3.9 Backstamp MIJ.1.

3.12 Backstamp 07.7.

3.10 Backstamp 07.0.

3.13 Backstamp 14.0.

3.11 Backstamp 07.3.

3.14 Backstamp 15.01.

3.15 Backstamp 16.0.

3.21 Backstamp 19.2.

3.22 Backstamp 21.0.

3.16 Backstamp 16.1.

3.23 Backstamp 24.1.

3.24 Backstamp 25.1.

3.17 Backstamp 16.4.

3.25 Backstamp 26.0.

3.26 Backstamp 26.1.

3.18 Backstamp 18.0.

3.20 Backstamp 19.1.

3.27 Backstamp 27.0.

3.28 Backstamp 27.1.

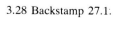

3.19 Backstamp 19.0.

3.29 Backstamp 27.2.

PART TWO

Introduction

To use Part Two of this book effectively, one needs to know only that the photo captions have five elements sequenced as follows:

Picture Number. Description (including comments, if any). Dimensions. Backstamp. Value.

Although these caption elements are largely self-explanatory, certain matters are reviewed below using sample captions.

L.21. Night light. 12.5"h x 7.0"w x 6.25"d. Backstamp: 27.0. $2000+

L.21A. Night light in L.21 illuminated.

P.12. Cake plate. 9.75"w x 9.5"d. Backstamp: 27.1. $60-80.

V.69. Vases. 8.5"h x 5.25"w. Backstamp: 27.0. $150-190.

V.69A. Detail of V.69, *left*. Compare the brush stroke details in this photo with those in V.69A; doing so should make it clear these two vases were entirely handpainted.

V.69B. Detail of V.69, *right*.

Picture Number

Each picture number is a combination of letters and numerals. First is a letter, which is the same one used to designate the chapter in which the photo appears. The letter has mnemonic value vis a vis the pieces shown in the chapter. Next are numerals which designate the sequential position of the picture in that chapter. Thus, a number such as "L.21" would designate the twenty-first photo in the "L" or "Lamps, Night Lights and Candleholders" chapter.

Sometimes there will be more than one photo of a piece, usually to show certain details more clearly or to provide another viewing perspective. Such photos are designated by letters which follow the numerals in this caption element. Thus, in the examples above, "L.21A" indicates a photo which is a variant of photo "L.21." In this instance, as the caption indicates, L.21A shows the night light in L.21 while it is lit. In the other example, above, there are two alternate photos: V.69A and V.69B. In this instance, these two photos are close-ups of each of the items in photo V.69.

Description (including comments, if any)

The words immediately following the photograph number indicate what an item is. In most instances, these words will be the same as one of the subgroup categories listed at the start of each chapter. If there are additional comments about the items shown, they are also inserted at this point in the caption. In the example above, there is such a comment with V.69A, although it is evident from reading it that the comment bears on V.69 and V.69B as well.

Dimensions

Data about dimensions are, by their very nature, approximate. For two reasons, it should not be assumed that other pieces like the ones shown in this book will exhibit exactly the same dimensions. First, variations in size can be expected when items are made of porcelain, because of both the character of porcelain and of the techniques used to create these particular pieces. Second, measurement errors are unavoidable even though every reasonable effort has been made to be as precise as possible about dimensions.

Dimensions are given in decimal form to the nearest eighth inch (0.13"). Normally, the first dimension given is overall, or greatest, height (indicated by the letter "h"). This is followed by overall width ("w") and, if available or useful, depth ("d"). In the examples above, this is illustrated by photo L.21.

Diameter (indicated by "dia.") is given only for basically flat items such as certain plates without handles, powder puff boxes, and the like. For objects that are *nearly* round, such as cake plates with small handles or some vases or jars, the dimensions given are "width" (at the widest point) and "depth" (i.e., the "other width") across the plate at a point without the handles. For example, in photo P.12 above, the dimensional numbers indicate that the "width" at the handles (9.75"w) is 0.25" greater than the "depth" (9.5"d–i.e., the "other width" without the handles).

Backstamp

The identity of most of the backstamps on pieces shown in this book is indicated by the word "Backstamp" followed by a number with 2 digits to the left of the decimal and from 1 to 3 to the right of it. By far the vast majority of the pieces in this book will have one of three kinds of backstamp:

1. an "M-in-Wreath" type (these are all designated by a number beginning with 2; indeed, about 90% of these will be 27.0 or 27.1)

2. a "Komaru" type (usually designated by the number 16.0, 16.1, etc.)

3.15 Backstamp 16.0.

3.21 Backstamp 19.2.

3.22 Backstamp 21.0.

3.16 Backstamp 16.1.

3.17 Backstamp 16.4.

3.24 Backstamp 25.1.

3.23 Backstamp 24.1.

3.18 Backstamp 18.0.

3.25 Backstamp 26.0.

3.26 Backstamp 26.1.

3.20 Backstamp 19.1.

3.19 Backstamp 19.0.

3.27 Backstamp 27.0.

3.28 Backstamp 27.1.

3.29 Backstamp 27.2.

3.30 Backstamp 27.3.

3.31 Backstamp 28.1.

3.32 Backstamp 28.1 (Roseara).

3.34 Backstamp 29.1 (19322).

3.33 Backstamp 29.1.

3.35 Backstamp 29.1 (29812).

3.36 Backstamp 33.056.

3.37 Backstamp 38.1.

3.38 Backstamp 39.019.

3.40 Backstamp 54.0.

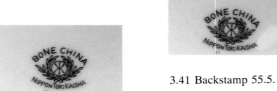

3.39 Backstamp 50.3.

3.42 Backstamp 56.15.

3.41 Backstamp 55.5.

3.43 Backstamp 64.019.

3.44 Backstamp 65.019.

3.45 Backstamp 65.5.

3.46 Backstamp 66.57.

3.47 Backstamp 67.019.

3.48 Backstamp 70.7.

3.49 Backstamp 70.7 (Mother's Day 1976, third edition, one of 2800).

3.50 Backstamp 71.7 (a limited edition of 10,000).

3.51 Backstamp 72.7.

3.52 Backstamp 74.5.

3.53 Backstamp 76.3.

3.54 Backstamp 77.3.

3.55 Backstamp 78.9.

3.56 Backstamp 86.5.

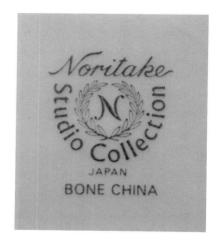

PART TWO

Introduction

To use Part Two of this book effectively, one needs to know only that the photo captions have five elements sequenced as follows:

Picture Number. Description (including comments, if any). Dimensions. Backstamp. Value.

Although these caption elements are largely self-explanatory, certain matters are reviewed below using sample captions.

L.21. Night light. 12.5"h x 7.0"w x 6.25"d. Backstamp: 27.0. $2000+

L.21A. Night light in L.21 illuminated.

P.12. Cake plate. 9.75"w x 9.5"d. Backstamp: 27.1. $60-80.

V.69. Vases. 8.5"h x 5.25"w. Backstamp: 27.0. $150-190.

V.69A. Detail of V.69, *left*. Compare the brush stroke details in this photo with those in V.69A; doing so should make it clear these two vases were entirely handpainted.

V.69B. Detail of V.69, *right*.

Picture Number

Each picture number is a combination of letters and numerals. First is a letter, which is the same one used to designate the chapter in which the photo appears. The letter has mnemonic value vis a vis the pieces shown in the chapter. Next are numerals which designate the sequential position of the picture in that chapter. Thus, a number such as "L.21" would designate the twenty-first photo in the "L" or "Lamps, Night Lights and Candleholders" chapter.

Sometimes there will be more than one photo of a piece, usually to show certain details more clearly or to provide another viewing perspective. Such photos are designated by letters which follow the numerals in this caption element. Thus, in the examples above, "L.21A" indicates a photo which is a variant of photo "L.21." In this instance, as the caption indicates, L.21A shows the night light in L.21 while it is lit. In the other example, above, there are two alternate photos: V.69A and V.69B. In this instance, these two photos are close-ups of each of the items in photo V.69.

Description (including comments, if any)

The words immediately following the photograph number indicate what an item is. In most instances, these words will be the same as one of the subgroup categories listed at the start of each chapter. If there are additional comments about the items shown, they are also inserted at this point in the caption. In the example above, there is such a comment with V.69A, although it is evident from reading it that the comment bears on V.69 and V69B as well.

Dimensions

Data about dimensions are, by their very nature, approximate. For two reasons, it should not be assumed that other pieces like the ones shown in this book will exhibit exactly the same dimensions. First, variations in size can be expected when items are made of porcelain, because of both the character of porcelain and of the techniques used to create these particular pieces. Second, measurement errors are unavoidable even though every reasonable effort has been made to be as precise as possible about dimensions.

Dimensions are given in decimal form to the nearest eighth inch (0.13"). Normally, the first dimension given is overall, or greatest, height (indicated by the letter "h"). This is followed by overall width ("w") and, if available or useful, depth ("d"). In the examples above, this is illustrated by photo L.21.

Diameter (indicated by "dia.") is given only for basically flat items such as certain plates without handles, powder puff boxes, and the like. For objects that are *nearly* round, such as cake plates with small handles or some vases or jars, the dimensions given are "width" (at the widest point) and "depth" (i.e., the "other width") across the plate at a point without the handles. For example, in photo P.12 above, the dimensional numbers indicate that the "width" at the handles (9.75"w) is 0.25" greater than the "depth" (9.5"d–i.e., the "other width" without the handles).

Backstamp

The identity of most of the backstamps on pieces shown in this book is indicated by the word "Backstamp" followed by a number with 2 digits to the left of the decimal and from 1 to 3 to the right of it. By far the vast majority of the pieces in this book will have one of three kinds of backstamp:

1. an "M-in-Wreath" type (these are all designated by a number beginning with 2; indeed, about 90% of these will be 27.0 or 27.1)

2. a "Komaru" type (usually designated by the number 16.0, 16.1, etc.)

3. a "Cherry Blossom" type (usually designated by the number 19.0, 19.1, etc.)

The number to the right of the decimal indicates the color of the backstamp. The four most commonly seen colors are: green (.0), red or maroon (.1), blue (.2), magenta (.3), teal (.4). Thus, the number 27.1 in the P.12 caption above would be read as indicating that the cake plate shown has a red (or maroon) "M-in-Wreath" backstamp. Other colors found on other backstamps are designated by other numerals to the right of the decimal. This topic is discussed in greater detail in Chapter 3 (p. 31).

Value

The last group of numbers in the caption indicate the *approximate retail value range* in current U.S. dollars of the items depicted. Thus, in example V.69 above, $150-190 would indicate an *approximate retail value range* of U.S. $150.00-$190.00. Sometimes, both ends of the range are *not* indicated numerically. Instead, just the lower end of the range is given. In L.21, for example, "$2000+" indicates that one could expect to see a retail price of *at least* $2000.00 on such a piece. This method of indicating value is reserved for rather unusual items which, so far, have been seen rarely if ever in the Noritake collectibles market.

It is impossible for the value designations to be any more than a *rough guide* to the current retail value of any of the pieces in this book. The condition of the piece (presumed to be "mint" in this book), individual preferences, changing fashions, and many other factors can have a significant impact on the utility of this information. Neither the publisher nor author is responsible for gains or losses that may occur when using or quoting the opinions expressed in this book.

Chapter A
Ashtrays and Other Items Pertaining to Smoking

In this chapter are photographs of items directly related in one way or another to smoking. Items are arranged in the order given:

Ashtrays (pp. 44-56)
Cigarette boxes (pp. 56-57)
Cigarette holders (pp. 57-59)
Cigarette jars (pp. 59-61)
Humidors (pp. 61-66)
Match holders (p. 66)
Pipe stand (p. 67)
Smoke sets (pp. 67-68)
Tobacco jars (p. 68)

Not until the 1920s was it widely fashionable for women to smoke. This development is reflected in the smoking items produced by the Noritake Company during and after this decade. In contrast to the more masculine colors and themes in the smoke sets, ashtrays, and humidors of the pre-1921 "Nippon" era, a great many items in this chapter, many from the latter half of the 1920s, incorporate distinctly feminine colors and subjects, including women themselves. In addition to providing hints about clothing, hair, and other fashion trends of the era, the motifs provide views of women engaging in an array of activities including golf, ice-skating, and horseback riding, which were signs of other more important emancipatory developments taking place in the lives of European and North American women at the time.

Another theme depicted in these pieces is the social nature of smoking. Men and women smoked at parties, while engaged in conversations with each other. These smoking items also point, albeit indirectly, to another feature of the 1920s era: the game of bridge. By the late 1920s, contract bridge had became a popular leisure activity for many people. For many, smoking and playing bridge was a "natural" combination. This is reflected in four-piece ashtray sets, featuring the four playing card suits. As demonstrated in this chapter, a few of these pieces may still be found in their original boxes.

The mention of such sets raises the question of the "definition" of an ashtray. In this book, items generally are not considered "ashtrays" unless they have at least one *distinct* cigarette rest (usually a groove of some sort at the edge of the tray). Most will find this viewpoint reasonable, but bridge sets demonstrate conclusively that one must not apply this principle too strictly. In one of the three bridge-ashtray sets in this chapter, two of the trays have no distinct cigarette rest. Clearly, then, it is not absolutely the case that a rest must be present for a "dish" to be considered an ashtray. As smokers and friends of smokers know quite well, a great variety of things can be and are used quite suitably as ashtrays.

Accordingly, some readers may find that an "ashtray" in their collection is shown in other chapters of this book (e.g., desk and dresser items or even bowls and boxes). In some cases, it may be argued that the piece should have been placed in this chapter. Ultimately, this is a judgment call, because for many items, there was no "true" function. Rather, it would seem that some items were intended to have multiple potential uses. In most cases, however, it should be clear that the lack of a defined cigarette rest makes it doubtful that the primary intended purpose of the piece was as an ashtray.

An important similar point must be made about what one often refers to as "dresser dolls." As the Larkin Company catalogs demonstrate, "dresser doll" is a legitimate term used for items sold apparently for various uses on dressers. In some cases, however, it does seem fairly clear that some "dresser dolls" were intended primarily for storing and serving cigarettes. Two primary clues support this claim. First, these containers, when figural in form, depict a female holding a cigarette. Second, the bottom half of such jars are tall and small enough to hold cigarettes easily but not other "dresser" items, such as powder. Thus, some items in this chapter will look similar to items that collectors have traditionally referred to as "dresser dolls."

A.1 Ashtray. 4.0"h x 6.0"dia. Backstamp: 27.0. $490-550.

A.1A Detail of Photo A.1.

A.2 Ashtray. 4.0"h x 6.0"dia. Backstamp: 27.0. $550-590.

A.4 Ashtray. 3.75"h x 5.25"w x 4.75"d. Backstamp: 27.0. $420-460.

A.3 Ashtray. 3.75"h x 5.13"w x 4.25"d. Backstamp: 27.0. $390-440.

A.3A Detail of Photo A.3.

A.5 Ashtrays. 2.13"h x 2.75"w. Backstamp: 27.1. Each, $230-270.

A.8 Ashtray. 2.0" h x 4.0"dia. Backstamp: 16.0. $160-190.

A.9 Ashtray. 1.5"h x 3.5"w. Backstamp: 27.0. $70-90.

A.6 Ashtray. 2.75"h x 4.75"dia. Backstamp: 27.0. $180-230.

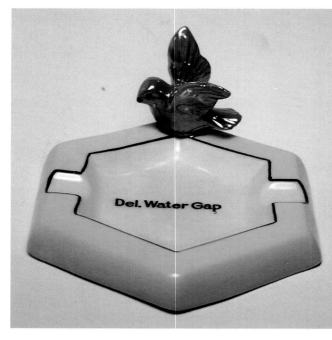

A.7 Ashtray. 2.75"h x 5.0"dia. Backstamp: 27.1. $160-190.

A.10 Ashtray. 2.75"h x 4.5"w x 3.63"d. Backstamp: 27.1. $190-230.

A.12 Ashtray. 2.75"h x 5.0"dia. Backstamp: 27.0. $150-190.

A.13 Ashtray. 2.5"h x 3.5"dia. Backstamp: 27.0. $180-230.

A.10A Reverse of photo A.10.

A.11 Ashtray. 2.75"h x 5.0"dia. Backstamp: 27.0. $150-190.

A.14 Ashtray. 2.5"h x 4.25"w x 1.13"d. Backstamp: 27.1. $190-280.

A.15 Ashtray. 2.5"h x 4.5"w. 16.2 $220-260.

A.16 Ashtray set. Ashtrays, 0.75"h x 2.75"w x 1.5"d. Box, 5.75"w x 3.75"d. Backstamp: 27.1. Set, $130-180.

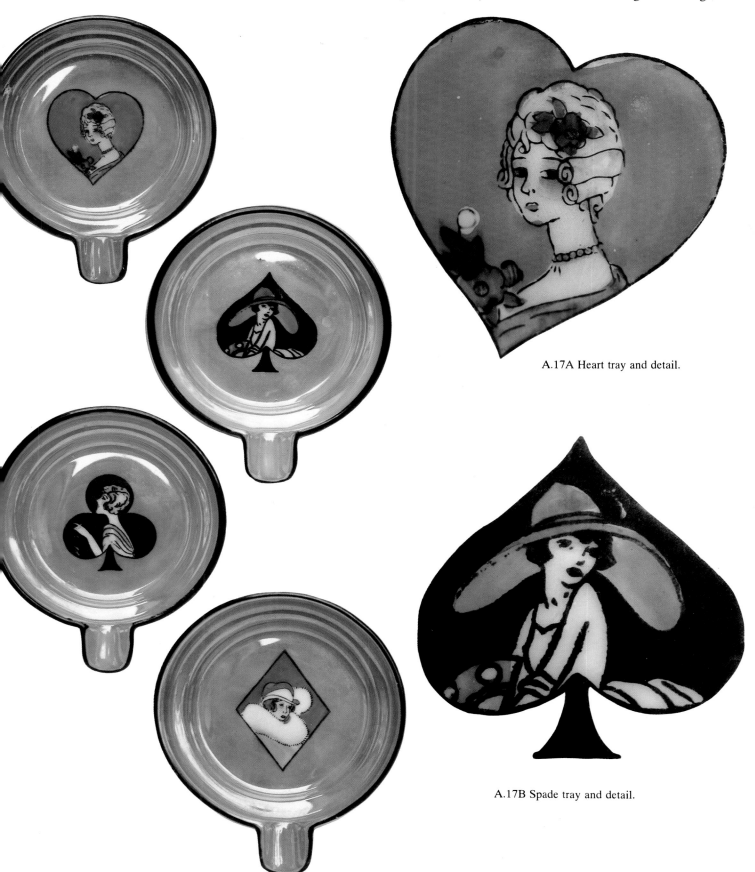

A.17A Heart tray and detail.

A.17B Spade tray and detail.

A.17 Ashtray set. 0.75"h x 2.88"w. Backstamp: 27.1. Four pieces, $300-350.

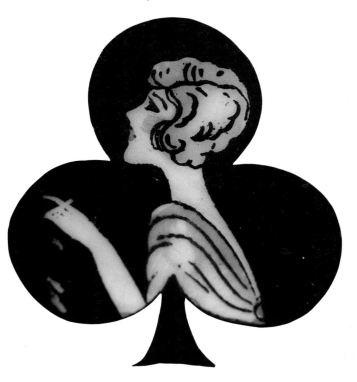

A.17C Club tray and detail.

A.18 Ashtray set. Box, 6.5"w x 6.5"d. Backstamp: 27.1. $90-130.

A.17D Diamond tray and detail.

A.19 Ashtray. 5.25"dia. Backstamp: 27.0. $200-250.

A.20 Ashtray. 2.0"h x 5.13"w. Backstamp: 27.0. $100-150.

A.23 Ashtray. 0.75"h x 4.25"dia. Backstamp: 27.0. $70-100.

A.24 Ashtray. 1.0"h x 5.38"w. Backstamp: 27.0. $120-180.

A.21 Ashtray. 2.0"h x 5.13"w. Backstamp: 27.0. $180-230.

A.22 Ashtray. 5.25"dia. Backstamp: 27.0. $230-280.

A.25 Ashtray. 2.25"h x 6.5"dia. Backstamp: 27.0. $60-100.

A.28 Ashtray. 1.13"h x 6.63"w x 6.0"d. Backstamp: 27.1. $160-190.

A.26 Ashtray. 1.13"h x 6.63"w x 6.0"d. Backstamp: 27.0. $150-180.

A.28A Detail of A.28.

A.27 Ashtray. 1.13"h x 6.63"w x 6.0"d. Backstamp: 27.0. $150-180.

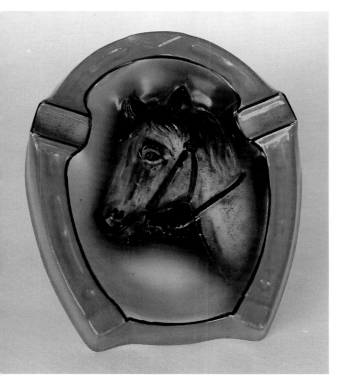

A.31 Ashtray. 2.0"h x 8.0"w x 6.63"d. Backstamp: 27.0. $280-320.

A.29 Ashtray. 1.25"h x 5.5"w x 4.5"d.
Backstamp: 27.0. $150-180.

A.30 Ashtray. 3.25"h x 5.0"w. Backstamp: 27.1. $90-120.

A.31A Top view of A.31.

A.32 Ashtray. 1.13"h x 6.25"w. Backstamp: 27.0.
$90-120.

A.33 Ashtray and match holder. 1.88"h x 2.75"w. Backstamp: 29.1. $190-240.

A.35 Ashtray and match holder. 2.0"h x 3.75"W x 3.75"d. Backstamp: 27.1. $250-300.

A.33A Reverse of A.33.

A.36 Ashtray and Cigarette cup. Ashtray, 4.5"w x 3.0"d. Cigarette cup, 2.25"h x 2.25"dia. Backstamp: 07.0. Set, $70-90.

A.34 Ashtray and match holder. 2.5"h x 3.75"w. Backstamp: 27.1. $80-100.

A.37 Ashtray and match holder. 2.0"h x 3.75"w x 2.75"d. Backstamp: 27.1. $180-230.

A.38 Ashtray. 1.0"h x 4.0"w x 3.63"d. Backstamp: 27.0. $90-120.

A.39 Ashtray. 1.25"h x 5.0"w. Backstamp: 27.0. $60-70.

A.37A Detail of A.37.

A.40 Ashtray. 4.75"h x 3.0"w x 1.88"d. Backstamp: 27.0. $70-90.

A.43 Cigarette box. 1.75"h x 3.5"w x 2.75"d.
Backstamp: 27.1. $440-490.

A.44 Cigarette box. 4.0"h x
3.5"w x 1.75"d. Backstamp:
29.1 (33519). $150-200.

A.41 Ashtray. 3.5"w x 3.25"d. Backstamp: 27.0. $100-150.

A.42 Cigarette box. 1.75"h x 3.5"w x 2.75"d. Backstamp: 27.1.
$380-430.

A.45 Cigarette box. 3.5"h x 2.63"w x 2.63"d. Backstamp: 27.1. $100-140.

A.48 Cigarette holder. 3.88"h x 3.25"w. Backstamp: 27.1. $80-120.

A.46 Cigarette holder. 3.75"h x 3.88"w. Backstamp: 27.1. $230-270.

A.47 Cigarette holder. 4.0"h x 3.0"w. Backstamp: 27.1. $230-270.

A.52 Cigarette holder. 4.0"h x 2.5"w x 1.88"d. Backstamp: MIJ.0. $200-250.

A.49 Cigarette holder. 3.0"h x 2.63"w. Backstamp: 27.1. $180-220.

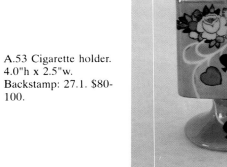

A.53 Cigarette holder. 4.0"h x 2.5"w. Backstamp: 27.1. $80-100.

A.50 Cigarette holders. 3.0"h x 2.38"w. Backstamp: 27.1. Each, $40-50.

A.51 Cigarette holder. 4.5"h x 3.0"w. Backstamp: 27.1. $80-120.

A.54 Cigarette holder. 3.88"h x 2.5"w.
Backstamp: 14.0. $60-90.

A.56 Cigarette jars. 5.75"h x 2.75"w. Backstamp: 27.1. Each, $380-420.

A.56A Detail of A.56.

A.55 Cigarette jar. 5.75"h x 2.75"w. Backstamp:
29.1 (29812). $380-420.

A.57 Cigarette jars. 5.75"h x 2.75"w. *Left,* Backstamp: 27.1. *Right,* Backstamp: 29.1 (25920). Each, $380-420.

A.59 Cigarette jar. 4.75"h x 3.5"w. Backstamp: 27.1. $280-330.

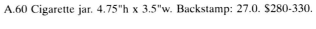

A.60 Cigarette jar. 4.75"h x 3.5"w. Backstamp: 27.0. $280-330.

A.58 Cigarette jars. 6.25"h x 3.0"w. *Left,* Backstamp: 29.1 (29812). *Right,* Backstamp: 27.1. Each, $420-460.

A.61 Cigarette jar. 4.75"h x 3.5"w. Backstamp: 27.0. $170-220.

A.62 Cigarette jar. 4.75"h x 3.5"w. Backstamp: 27.1. $130-170.

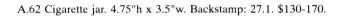

A.63 Humidor. 6.75"h x 5.0"w. Backstamp: 27.1. $650-690.

A.64 Humidors. 6.75"h x 5.0"w x 5.0"d. *Left*, Backstamp: 27.1. *Right*, Backstamp: 19.1 Each, $630-660.

A.65 Humidor. 7.25"h x 5.5"w. Backstamp: 27.0. $630-660.

A.66 Humidor. 6.75"h x 4.25"w. Backstamp: 27.0. $630-660.

A.67 Humidor. 6.63"h x 4.5"w. Backstamp: 27.0. $530-590.

A.67A Detail of back of A.67.

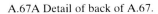

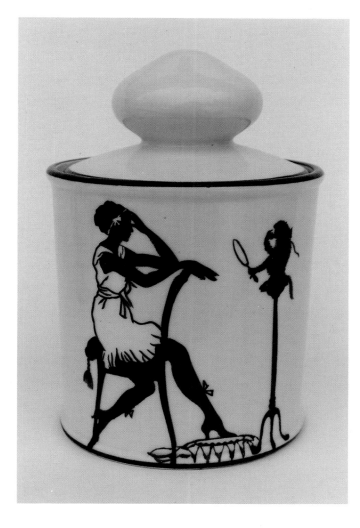

A.70 Humidor.
6.63"h x 4.5"w.
Backstamp: 27.0.
$520-580.

A.68 Humidor. 6.63"h x 4.5"w. Backstamp: 27.0. $530-590.

A.71 Humidor. 6.63"h x 4.5"w. Backstamp: 27.0. $420-470.

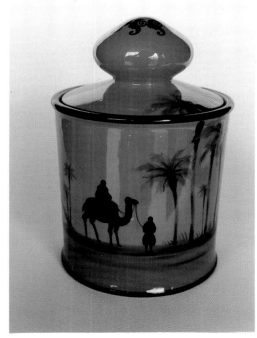

A.69 Humidor. 6.63"h x 4.5"w.
Backstamp: 27.0. $520-580.

A.72 Humidor. 6.63"h x 4.5"w. Backstamp: 27.0.
$350-390.

A.74 Humidor. 6.25"h x 5.5"w. Backstamp: 27.0. $330-360.

A.73 Humidor. 6.25"h x 5.5"w. Backstamp: 27.0. $350-390.

A.75 Humidor. 6.25"h x 5.5"w. Backstamp: 27.0. $330-360.

A.76 Humidor. 6.0"h x 5.88"w. Backstamp: 27.0. $300-350.

A.79 Humidor.
5.5"h x 4.25"w.
Backstamp: 18.0.
$200-250.

A.77 Humidor. 5.75"h x 5.5"w. Backstamp: 27.0. $300-350.

A.80 Humidor.
5.5"h x 4.25"w.
Backstamp: 19.3.
$200-250.

A.78 Humidor. 5.75"h x 5.5"w. Backstamp: 27.0. $250-300.

A.83 Match holder. 3.5"h x 3.75"w. Backstamp: 27.0. $90-120.

A.81 5.38"h x 4.25"w. Backstamp: 21.0. $300-350.

A.82 Match holder. 2.5"h x 1.88"w x 1.13"d. Backstamp: 27.1. $160-200.

A.84 Match holder. 3.5"h x 3.75"w. Backstamp: 27.0. $110-160.

A.85 Match holder. 3.5"h x 3.75"w. Backstamp: 26.0. $80-100.

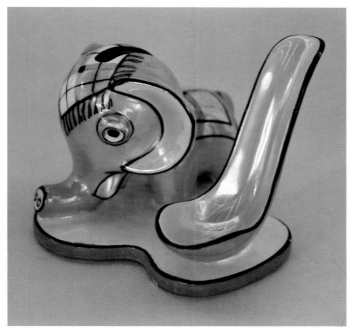

A.86 Pipe stand. 2.75"h x 3.75"w. Backstamp: 27.1. $400+

A.89 Smoke set. Tray has no backstamp; cup has full backstamp; match holder has backstamp MIJ.1. Tray, 6.75"w. Match holder, 2.25"h. Cup, 2.25"h x 2.25"dia. Backstamp: 27.1. $250-300.

A.87 Smoke set. All three pieces have full backstamp; box is larger than usual cigarette box. Tray, 5.0" x 7.5". Box, 1.5"h x 3.75"w x 3.0"d. Backstamp: 27.1. $400-500.

A.90 Smoke set. 2.25"h x 7.0"w. Backstamp: 27.1. $280-330.

A.88 Smoke set. Tray, 0.38"h x 8.0"w x 5.0"d. Box, 1.5"h x 3.75"w x 3.0"d. Ashtray, 2.0"h x 3.25"w. Backstamp: 27.1. $230-290.

A.91 Smoke set. 2.0"h x 4.5"w. Backstamp: 27.1. $140-160.

A.94 Tobacco jar. 5.5"h x 3.5"w. Backstamp: 27.0. $190-240.

A.92 Smoke set tray. 0.38"h x 7.63"dia. Backstamp: 27.0. $160-200.

A.95 Tobacco jar. 3.75"h x 3.5"w. Backstamp: 27.0. $120-190.

A.93 Tobacco jar. 4.25"h x 3.75"w. Backstamp: 27.1. $240-300.

Bowls and Boxes

In this chapter, there are photos of nearly 200 Noritake bowls and boxes. Some sense of the order imposed on this diverse array of items may be gained by examining the list of subgroups below. The rationale for and information about these subgroups is presented in the paragraphs following the list.

Bowls
1. "Gemini" & "Sisters" bowls (pp. 70-71)
2. General purpose bowls
    Bowls with no handles (pp.. 72-78)
        Round bowls (pp. 72-73)
        Sided bowls (pp.73-78)
    Bowls with one handle (pp. 79-89)
        Basket bowls (pp. 79-84)
        Bowls with figural birds (pp 85-87)
        Other bowls with one handle (pp. 87-89)
    Bowls with two handles (pp 90-104)
    Bowls with three or four handles (pp. 104-106)
3. Special purpose bowls
    Celery and relish bowls (pp. 107-108)
    Compotes (pp. 108-113)
        Compotes with handles (pp. 108-111)
        Compotes without handles (pp. 111-113)
    Covered bowls (pp. 114-115)
    Nut bowls (pp. 116-117)
    Punch bowls (p. 117)
    Salad bowls (p. 118)

Boxes
1. Figural covered boxes (pp. 118-120)
2. Other covered boxes (pp. 120-123)

As previously noted, one of my main objectives for this book was to make it "user friendly;" I wanted readers to be able to find things of interest to them *quickly*. This effort was put to the greatest test while I was organizing the pieces in this chapter. Many potential subgroups were contemplated. Many were based on common shapes and motifs (e.g., florals, geometrics, ladies, animals, etc.). Some of these methods yielded subgroups which were interesting aesthetically or otherwise. It became obvious, however, that such groups would not be useful in this chapter. First, the motif-based systems rested upon the assumption that readers would easily guess in which subgroup I had placed a bowl. Second, many of the shape-based systems were both too complex and ambiguous.

After trying numerous options, a system with just a few simple rules was adopted. With it, a small number of easily distinguished basic "kinds" of bowls and boxes was generated. In *this* chapter (boxes associated clearly with smoking, as well as with dresser and desk uses are shown in Chapters A and D, respectively), two kinds of boxes are distinguished: 1) figural covered boxes and 2) all other covered boxes (other than those indicated previously). Two *broad* kinds of bowls are distinguished in this chapter: 1) general purpose bowls and 2) special purpose bowls. Salad bowls, nut bowls, celery/relish bowls, and punch bowls are examples of the latter kind; the function of such bowls can be seen easily by noting their shapes and/or decoration. Two other bowl varieties have been designated in this book as special purpose bowls: 1) bowls with lids and 2) bowls on pedestals ("compotes" or "comports").

There are more than 100 general purpose bowls in this chapter and, had there been more space, there could easily have been *far* more. Because there are so many, a *simple* method for creating subgroups was needed. Four subgroups were created using one easily remembered feature of bowls–the number of handles. Because this principle yielded two rather large subgroups (bowls with no handles and bowls with one handle), these subgroups were further subdivided in terms of basic shape (i.e, whether a bowl with no handle was round or not) and kind of handle (in the case of one-handled bowls).

Within all of the subgroups and the sub-subgroups, items are generally sequenced in terms of overall size, from large to small, with two main exceptions. The sided bowls are sequenced by the number of sides, and bowls of varying size but similar shape (or "blank") are grouped together even if some of the bowls in such a sequence are smaller than subsequent bowls of different shape.

With this system, the reader can easily and quickly find nearly any bowl in the chapter. The reader must first decide whether or not the bowl in question has a special purpose. If it is a special purpose bowl, they can refer to pages with that kind of bowl. If it is not a special purpose bowl, it must then be noted whether the bowl is round or sided if it has no handles; whether it has a basket-type handle, figural bird handle, or some other type of handle (if only one handle); or whether the bowl has two, three, or four handles, if more than one handle. To the best of my knowledge, only one bowl in this chapter is located in a way that violates these rules. This bowl (photo B.37) has two basket handles but is grouped with the other basket-handled bowls, all of which have just one handle.

This is not to say that there can be no debate about the way materials have been grouped. This is partly because words like "box," "bowl," "jar," and "basket," although used frequently and with great confidence, are not easily defined unambiguously. As a result, it can be expected that others will doubt the usage. In light of this, additional comments about the character of and rationale for each of the subgroups follows.

The "Gemini" & "Sisters" Bowls

If it were not so corny, one could refer to these as the Noritake "super bowls." Although "out of order," given the alphabetical organization of the materials in this chapter, these bowls deserve special recognition, expecially in a chapter that is so large. Known by the names indicated in the captions, these items are widely admired and sought after by collectors. I hope the reader will excuse this personal indulgence on my part. I can only say in defense that none of these particular bowls are mine nor do I have any like them. It may also be worth emphasizing, in this context, that there are many other items in this chapter which quite a few collectors would value at least as highly as these particular bowls. Ultimately, in such matters, personal preference reigns supreme.

B.1 Three bowls. *Upper*, "Gemini" bowl. 6.13"h x 6.63"w x 5.0"d.
Backstamp: 27.1. $1500-1800. *Lower*, "Sisters" bowls. 4.0"h x
8.0"w x 5.25"d. Backstamp: 27.1. Each, $1300-1500.

B.2 Gemini bowl. 6.13"h x 6.63"w x 5.0"d. Backstamp: 27.1.
$1500-1800.

B.3 Gemini bowl. 6.13"h x 6.63"w x 5.0"d. Backstamp: 16.0.
$1500-1800.

B.4 Sisters bowl. 4.0"h x 8.0"w x 5.25"d. Backstamp: 27.1. $1300-1500.

B.5 Sisters bowl. 4.0"h x 8.0"w x 5.25"d. Backstamp: 27.1. $1300-1500.

General Purpose Bowls

Bowls with no handles

This first subgroup of the bowls section of the chapter is subdivided into round bowls and sided bowls. A round bowl without handles may be thought of, in a sense, as the "quintessential bowl." Such bowls are a good starting point for the chapter. Round bowls are sequenced according to size, beginning with the largest. The term *sided bowls*, in this book, designates a bowl which, although often basically round, is not round in the simple or "pure" sense of the term. Instead, a sided bowl has sections or segments that, in terms of shape, approach the idea of "sides" without quite being "sides." Also included in this cluster are bowls basically rectangular or square in shape, which have been made more complex by the addition of numerous "points." The sided bowls for the most part have been sequenced by the number of their sides or quasi-sides.

B.9 Round bowl. 2.75"h x 9.75"w. Backstamp: 19.1. $90-110.

B.10 Round bowl. 2.75"h x 8.5"w. Backstamp: 27.0. $110-140.

B.6 Round bowl. 3.0"h x 8.88"w. Backstamp: 27.0. $90-120.

B.7 Round bowl. 3.0"h x 8.88"w. Backstamp: 27.0. $90-120.

B.8 Round bowl. 3.0"h x 8.88"w. Backstamp: 27.0. $80-100.

B.13 Round bowl. 2.5"h x 5.0"w. Backstamp: 26.1. $30-50.

B.11 Round bowl. 2.38"h x 9.5"w. Backstamp: 19.1. $60-90.

B.14 Sided bowl. 3.88"h x 7.0"w. Backstamp: 27.1. $90-130.

B.12 Round bowl. 3.25"h x 5.25"w. Backstamp: 27.4. $40-50.

B.15 Sided bowl. 2.88"h x 8.0"w. Backstamp: 16.0. $160-200.

B.17 Sided bowl. 2.0"h x 4.75"dia. Backstamp: 15.01 (44046). $40-60.

B.18 Sided bowl. 2.0"h x 7.0"w. Backstamp: 25.1. $50-60.

B.15B Top view of B.15.

B.16 Sided bowl. 3.75"h x 10.0"w x 8.38"d.
Backstamp: 27.0. $80-100.

B.19 Sided bow. 1.75"h x 7.63"w. Backstamp: 28.1. $70-90.

B.22 Sided bowl. 2.0"h x 9.25"w. Backstamp: 19.1. $70-90.

B.20 Sided bowl. 2.13"h x 7.25"w x 6.75"d. Backstamp: 27.1. $250-300.

B.21 Sided bowl. 2.13"h x 7.25"w x 6.75"d. Backstamp: 26.1. $100-130.

B.23 Sided bowls. 3.0"h x 11.5"w x 8.5"d. *Left*, Backstamp: 27.1. $80-100. *Right*, Backstamp: 19.1. $80-100.

B.26 Sided bowl. This bowl has three feet. 1.63"h x 5.38"dia. Backstamp: 27.1. $30-50.

B.24 Sided bowl. This berry strainer has three short legs. 2.25"h x 7.75"dia. Backstamp: 16.0. $80-100.

B.25 Sided bowl. This bowl has three feet. 1.63"h x 5.5"dia. Backstamp: 25.1. $30-50.

B.27 Bowl. This bowl has three legs. 2.25"h x 4.75"dia. Backstamp: 24.1. $30-40.

B.29 Bowl. 3.75"h x 10.5"w. Backstamp: 27.1. $90-120.

B.28 Bowl. 3.75"h x 10.5"w. Backstamp: 27.1. $80-110.

B.30 Bowl. 2.13"h x 7.5" x 7.5"w. Backstamp: 27.1. $110-150.

B.28B A side view of B.28.

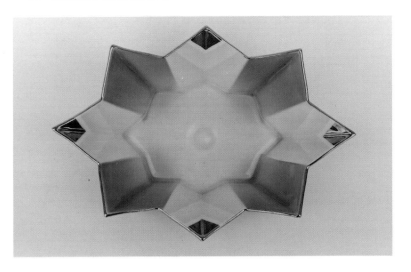

B.31 Bowl. 2.25"h x 9.75"w x 7.25"d. Backstamp: 27.1. $120-160.

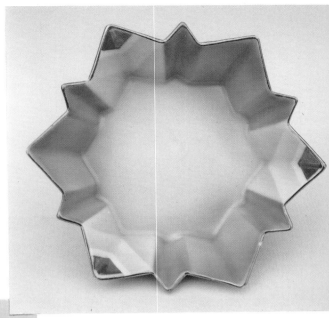

B.34 Bowl. 2.0"h x 6.5"w. Backstamp: 27.1. $80-100.

B.32 Bowl. 2.25"h x 9.75"w x 7.25"d. Backstamp: 27.1. $120-160.

B.35 Bowl. 2.38"h x 8.5"w. Backstamp: 27.1. $120-150.

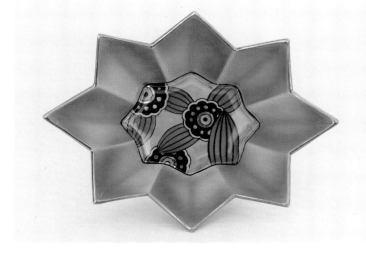

B.33 Bowl. 2.25"h x 7.25"w x 5.63"d. Backstamp: 27.1. $130-170.

B.38 Basket. 5.75"h x 8.38"d. 19.1 $90-130.

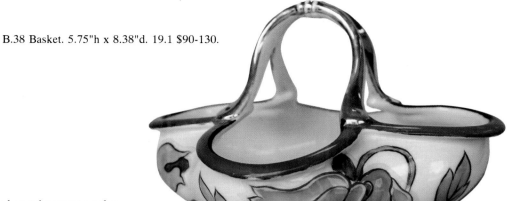

Bowls with one handle

This subgroup, like the previous one, has subgroups or clusters within it–in this case, basket bowls, bowls with figural birds, and other one-handled bowls. Basket bowls, with one exception noted above, have a single, relatively large handle which, because it runs across the piece, tends to make people think of the piece as a "basket." Because of their evident function, some very large baskets are found with vases in Chapter V. Bowls with figural birds, which can or were intended to serve as handles, constitute a distinct subgroup for most collectors and dealers; moreover, it is a fairly unambiguous group. Items with such handles are, therefore, clustered as a sub-subgroup within this chapter.

B.36 Basket. 4.0"h x 11.75"w x 4.88"d.
Backstamp: 27.1. $120-170.

B.37 Basket. 3.5"h x 8.5"w x 4.5"d. Backstamp:
27.1. $120-170.

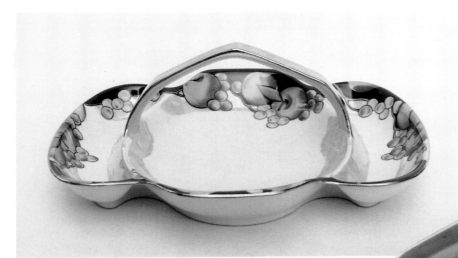

B.40 Basket. 3.13"h x 8.25"w x 7.0"d. Backstamp: 27.1. $80-100.

B.43 Basket. 3.63"h x 7.75"w. Backstamp: 14.0 (39539). $70-90.

B.41 Basket. 5.75"h x 8.0"w. Backstamp: 27.1. $120-170.

B.42 Basket. 5.75"h x 8.0"w. Backstamp: 21.0. $120-170.

B.44 Basket. 3.0"h x 7.63"w x 5.38"d.
Backstamp: 27.0. $60-90.

B.47 Basket. 4.0"h x 7.0"w. Backstamp: 27.1.
$40-60.

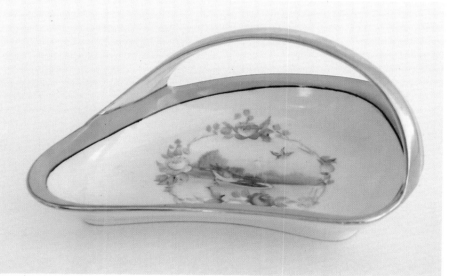

B.45 Basket. 3.75"h x 7.0"w. Backstamp: 27.0.
$60-90.

B.46 Basket. 4.0"h x 7.0"w. Backstamp: 27.1. $250-300.

B.48 Basket. 2.25"h x 7.0"w x 3.5"d. Backstamp: 27.0. $80-100.

B.50 Basket. 5.13"h x 6.75"w x 5.0"d. Backstamp: 27.1. $80-100.

B.51 Basket. 5.13"h x 6.75"w x 5.0"d.
Backstamp: 27.1. $80-100.

B.49 Basket. 5.5"h x 6.75"w. Backstamp: 27.1. $80-100.

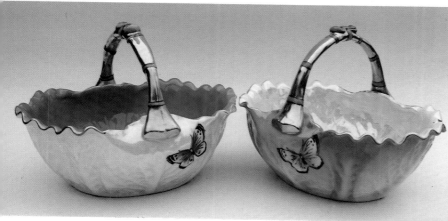

B.52 Baskets. 5.13"h x 6.75"w x 5.0" Backstamp: 27.1. Each, $80-100.

B.55 Basket. 5.25"h x 6.5"h x 4.5"d. Backstamp: 27.1. $70-90.

B.56 Basket. 4.5"h x 4.63"w. Backstamp: 27.1. $100-120.

B.53 Basket. 4.5"h x 6.5"w. Backstamp: 27.1. $110-130.

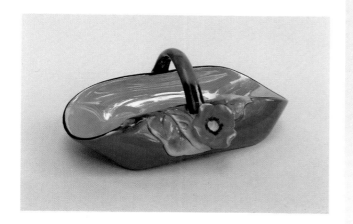

B.54 Basket. 2.75"h x 6.5"w x 4.75"d. Backstamp: 27.1. $70-90.

B.57 Basket. 4.63"h x 5.0"w x 4.25"d. Backstamp: 29.1. $70-100.

B.59 Basket. 4.75"h x 5.5"w. Backstamp: 27.1. $60-90.

B.58 Basket. 4.63"h x 5.0"w x 4.25"d. Backstamp: 27.1. $60-90.

B.60 Basket. 4.5"h x 3.75"w x 2.75"d. Backstamp: 29.1. $60-80.

B.61 Bowl with figural bird. 3.5"h x 9.5"w x 9.0"d. Backstamp: 27.1. $330-380.

B.64 Bowl with figural bird. 2.75"h x 7.5"w x 6.5"d. Backstamp: 27.1. $80-100.

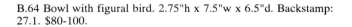

B.62 Bowl with figural bird. 4.0"h x 7.88"w x 5.5"d. Backstamp: 27.0. $130-150.

B.63 Bowl with figural bird. 2.5"h x 6.5"w x 5.75"d. Backstamp: 27.0. $60-80.

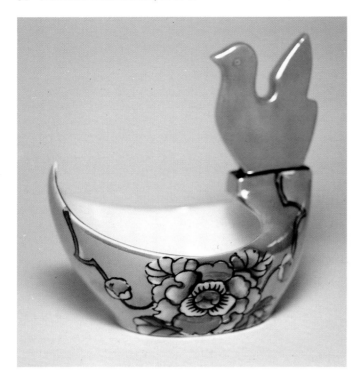

B.65 Bowl with figural bird. 5.0"h x 4.5"w x
3.5"d. Backstamp: 19.0. $170-190.

B.67 Bowl with figural bird. 5.0"h x 4.5"w x
3.5"d. Backstamp: 27.1. $170-190.

B.68 Bowl with figural bird. 5.0"h x 4.5"w x 3.5"d. Backstamp:
27.1. $80-100.

B.66 Bowl with figural bird. 5.0"h x 4.5"w x
3.5"d. Backstamp: 27.1. $170-190.

B.69 Bowls with figural bird. 5.0"h x 4.5"w x 3.5"d. Backstamp: 27.1. Each, $80-100.

B.72 Bowl with one handle. This bowl has three feet. Azalea Larkin #188. 3.63"h x 7.88"w. Backstamp: 29.1 (19322). $350-400.

B.70 Bowl with one handle. This bowl has three feet. 3.5"h x 9.75"w x 7.50"d. Backstamp: 19.1. $80-120.

B.71 Bowl with one handle. This bowl has three feet. 3.63"h x 7.88"w. Backstamp: 27.1. $180-225.

B.76 Bowl with one handle. 2.75"h x
6.75"w x 4.63"d. Backstamp: 27.1. $70-90.

B.73 Bowl with one handle. 4.25"h x 7.5"w. Backstamp: 27.1. $80-
100.

B.74 Bowl with one handle. 1.88"h x 8.13"w x 5.25"d.
Backstamp: 27.0. $30-40.

B.75 Bowl with one handle. 2.75"h x 6.75"w x 4.63"d. Backstamp:
27.1. $70-90.

B.80 Bowl with one handle. 1.5"h x 5.13"w x 4.88"d. Backstamp: 19.0. $20-40.

B.77 Bowl with one handle. 6.5"w x 5.0"d. Backstamp: 27.1. $30-40.

B.81 Bowl with one handle. 0.88"h x 5.0"w x 3.63"d. Backstamp: 27.1. $30-40.

B.78 Bowl with one handle. 1.5"h x 6.25"w x 4.75"d. Backstamp: 27.0. $20-30.

B.79 Bowl with one handle. 1.25"h x 5.88"w. Backstamp: 27.1. $60-90.

Bowls with two handles

Most of the bowls in this subgroup have two quite obvious handles. However, this subgroup also includes bowls which, at first glance, may appear to have four handles. If such bowls are examined closely, it will nearly always be clear that two of the four "handles" are clearly more "handle like;" for example, by virtue of pierced openings or other obvious distinctions.

B.84 Bowl with two handles. 1.5"h x 11.5"w x 5.38"d. Backstamp: 16.0. $50-70.

B.82 Bowl with two handles. 1.5"h x 12.5"w x 5.63"d. Backstamp: 27.1. $70-90.

B.83 Bowl with two handles. 3.0"h x 11.63"w x 7.63"d. Backstamp: 27.0. $180-200.

B.83A Detail of B.83.

B.85 Bowl with two handles. There are three different scenes painted on the inside of this bowl. 2.38"h x 10.75"w x 7.0"d. Backstamp: 27.0. $150-180.

B.86 Bowl with two handles. 1.75"h x 10.38"w x 10.0"d. Backstamp: 25.1. $90-130.

B.87 Bowl with two handles. 1.75"h x 10.38"w x 8.25"d. Backstamp: 27.0. $90-120.

B.87A Detail of B.87.

B.90 Bowl with two handles. 9.63"w x 8.25"d. Backstamp: 27.1. $100-150.

B.88 Bowl with two handles. 2.0"h x 10.25"w x 7.63"d. Backstamp: 27.0. $90-120.

B.90A Detail of B.90.

B.89 Bowl with two handles. 1.5"h x 8.5"w x 6.63"d. Backstamp: 27.0. $60-90.

B.91 Bowl with two handles. 2.25"h x 9.38"w x 9.13"d. Backstamp: 27.1. $90-130.

B.93A Detail of B.93.

B.92 Bowl with two handles. 2.25"h x 8.75"w x 7.25"d. Backstamp: 27.0. $100-140.

B.93 Bowl with two handles. 2.25"h x 8.0"w x 7.5"d. Backstamp: 16.2. $100-140.

B.94A Detail of B.94.

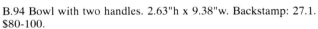

B.94 Bowl with two handles. 2.63"h x 9.38"w. Backstamp: 27.1.
$80-100.

B.96 Bowl with two handles.
2.5"h x 9.25"w x 8.0"d.
Backstamp: 19.1. $80-100.

B.95 Bowl with two handles. 2.0"h x 9.0"w x 7.88"d. Backstamp:
27.1. $80-90.

B.97 Bowl with two handles. 2.5"h x 9.13"w x 8.13"d. Backstamp: 27.0. $60-90.

B.99 Bowl with two handles. This bowl is unusual, in that it has two complete and different Noritake backstamps; see photo B.99A. 1.88"h x 8.88"w x 7.25"d Backstamp: 16.0. and 19.1. $30-60.

B.99A Backstamps on bowl in B.99. 0.5"h x 1.0"w.

B.98 Bowl with two handles. 1.88"h x 8.88"w x 7.25"d. Backstamp: 25.1. $50-70.

B.98A Detail of B.98.

B.100 Bowl with two handles. 1.75"h x 7.38"w x 6.0"d. Backstamp: 27.1. $80-100.

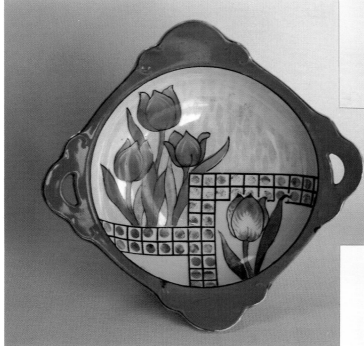

B.102 Bowl with two handles. 3.0"h x 8.75"w x 6.75"d. Backstamp: 27.0. $90-130.

B.102A View inside of bowl in B.102.

B.101 Bowl with two handles. 1.75"h x 7.38"w x 6.0"d. Backstamp: 27.1. $40-60.

B.103 Bowl with two handles. 1.25"h x 8.63"w x 5.25"d.
Backstamp: 27.0. $70-90.

B.103A Detail of B.103.

B.104A Detail of B.104.

B.104 Bowl with two handles. 2.5"h x 8.5"w x 8.5"d. Backstamp: 27.0. $120-160.

B.106 Bowl with two handles. 1.5"h x 8.5"h x 7.5"d. Backstamp: 27.1. $60-80.

B.105 Bowl with two handles. 2.0"h x 8.5"w x 8.0"d. Backstamp: 27.1. $90-120.

B.107 Bowl with two handles. 1.5"h x 8.13"h x 7.25"d. Backstamp: 27.1. $60-80.

B.108 Bowl with two handles. 2.0"h x 8.38"w x 8.13"d. Backstamp: 16.2. $60-90.

B.107A Detail of B.107.

B.109 Bowl with two handles. 1.75"h x 8.25"w x 7.38"d. Backstamp: 27.0. $50-70.

B.110 Bowl with two handles. 3.0"h x 8.25"w x 6.38"d. Backstamp: 29.1 (39556). $90-130.

B.110A Detail of B.110.

B.112 Bowl with two handles. 2.0"h x 8.0"h x 7.0"d. Backstamp: 27.0. $60-80.

B.111 Bowl with two handles. 2.0"h x 8.25"w x 7.13"d. Backstamp: 27.1. $50-60.

B.113 Bowl with two handles. 2.13"h x 8.0"w x 6.75"d. Backstamp: 27.1. $90-120.

B.116 Bowl with two handles. 2.5"h x 7.5"w x 6.38"d. Backstamp: 27.0. $60-90.

B.114 Bowl with two handles. 2.0"h x 8.0"w x 7.25"d. Backstamp: 27.1. $60-80.

B.115 Bowl with two handles. 2.0"h x 7.75"w x 4.25"d. Backstamp: 27.0. $50-60.

B.117 Bowl with two handles. 1.25"h x 7.5"w x
6.0"d. Backstamp: 27.0. $60-90.

B.119 Bowl with two handles. 1.88"h x 6.75"w
x 5.88"d. Backstamp: 27.1. $60-80.

B.117A Detail of B.117.

B.118 Bowl with two handles. 1.63"h x 7.25"w
x 6.75"d. Backstamp: 27.1. $40-60.

B.120 Bowl with two handles. 1.5"h x 6.5"w x 5.63"d. Backstamp: 27.0. $40-60.

B.122 Bowl with two handles. 1.75"h x 6.5"w x 5.5"d. Backstamp: 27.1. $80-100.

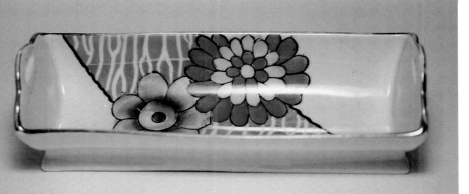

B.122A Detail of B.122.

B.121 Bowl with two handles. The shape of this unusual bowl suggests it may have been intended for serving crackers. 2.5"h x 7.0"w x 2.0"d. Backstamp: 27.1. $60-90.

B.123 Bowl with two handles. 0.75"h x 5.5"w x
4.63"d. Backstamp: 16.0. $30-40.

B.123A Shows detail of decal applied to piece in B.123.

Bowls with three or four handles

This subgrouping concludes the series of bowl subgroups
based on the number of handles. Because the number of the
bowls in neither of the potential clusters (three and four handles)
is large, this subgroup includes both. The bowls are, however,
generally sequenced first by number of handles and then by
size.

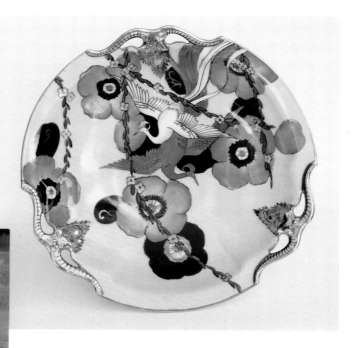

B.124 Three-handled bowl. 2.25"h x 9.5"w x
9.25"d. Backstamp: 27.1. $120-170.

B.124A Detail of B.124.

B.127 Three-handled bowl. 1.5"h x 8.0"w. Backstamp: 25.1. $60-80.

B.125 Three-handled bowl. 2.25"h x 9.5"w x 9.25"d. Backstamp: 27.1. $100-140.

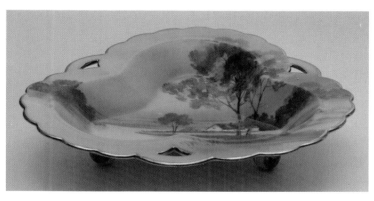

B.128 Three-handled bowl with feet. 1.63"h x 6.88"w. Backstamp: 27.0. $60-80.

B.126 Three-handled bowl. 2.0"h x 8.25"w. Backstamp: 27.0. $90-120.

B.126A Detail of B.126.

B.129 Three-handled bowl. 6.0"w x 6.0"d. Backstamp: 27.1. $80-100.

B.131 Four-handled bowl. 1.75"h x 6.5"w x 6.0"d. Backstamp: 25.1. $90-130.

B.130 Four-handled bowl. 2.5"h x 8.5"w x 8.0"d. Backstamp: 27.1. $90-130.

B.131A Detail of B.131

B.132 Four-handled bowl. 2.75"h x 7.5"w x 7.5"d. Backstamp: 27.1. $90-140.

Special Purpose Bowls

Celery and relish bowls

These bowls, which can have either one or two handles, ordinarily were decorated in a way that makes it easy for collectors and dealers to see what their intended use was. Accordingly, these pieces tend to be referred to generally in the trade as "celery or relish bowls." They are, therefore, separated into their own subgroup in this chapter.

B.133 Celery set. 2.25"h x 12.75"w. Backstamp: 27.1. Set, $120-180.

B.134 Celery set. 2.0"h x 12.0"w x 5.25"d. Backstamp: 27.0. Set, $80-100.

B.134A Detail of B.134.

Compotes

Compotes (also known as "comports," although this term has fallen into disuse) are essentially bowls set on a type of pedestal. As used in this book, "pedestal" is to be contrasted with "feet." Noritake compotes vary greatly in shape and size. Even so, they may be generally distinguished by whether or not they have handles. In this chapter, consequently, compotes are first subdivided according to whether they have handles and within each of these subgroups, they are sequenced in terms of size. For reasons noted below, some very large "compotes" of potential interest to readers may be grouped with "punch bowls."

B.135 Celery set. 12.0"w x 6.0"d. Backstamp: 27.0. Set, $80-120.

B.136 Celery set. 1.5"h x 11.5"w x 5.5"d. Backstamp: 28.1 (Roseara). Set, $80-100.

B.138 Compote with handles. 6.75"h x 12.0"w x 9.25"d. Backstamp: 27.0. $450+

B.137 Relish set. 2.5"h x 8.0"w x 5.25"d. Backstamp: 27.1. Set, $80-100.

B.139 Compote with handles. 3.25"h x 11.0"w x 9.5"d. Backstamp: 27.1. $120-180.

B.140A Detail of B.140.

B.140 Compote with handles. 2.63"h x 10.0"w x 8.0"d. Backstamp: 19.1 $100-130.

B.141 Compote with handles. 2.63"h x 10.0"w x 8.0"d. Backstamp: 27.1. $70-90.

B.141A Detail of B.141.

B.142 Compote with handles. 2.63"h x 8.63"w x 6.88"d. Backstamp: 27.0. $140-190.

B.142A Detail of B142.

B.145 Compote without handles. 6.75"h x 9.13"w. Backstamp: 27.0. $150-190.

B.143 Compote with handles. 2.25"h x 8.0"w x 6.63"d. Backstamp: 27.1. $70-90.

B.146 Compote without handles. Height of pedestal is 4.5". 6.75"h x 6.75"w. Backstamp: 27.1. $590-650.

B.144 Compote with handles. 2.25"h x 6.75"w x 5.75"d. Backstamp: 19.2. $70-90.

B.149 Compote without handles. 3.0"h x 8.75"w. Backstamp: 25.1. $150-200.

B.147 Compote without handles. 5.0"h x 7.13"w. Backstamp: 27.0. $90-120.

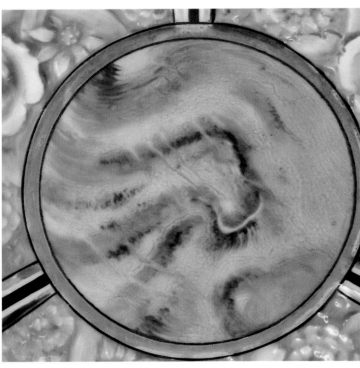

B.148 Compote without handles. 3.5"h x 9.0"w. Backstamp: 19.1. $60-80.

B.149A Detail of B.149.

B.148A Top of B.148.

B.150 Compote without handles. 3.0"h x 6.75"w. Backstamp: 27.1. $120-180.

B.153 Compote without handles. 2.75"h x 6.5"w. Backstamp: 27.0. $60-90.

B.151 Compote without handles. 3.0"h x 6.75"w. Backstamp: 27.1. $120-180.

B.154 Compote without handles. 2.88"h x 6.5"w. Backstamp: 19.0. $60-80.

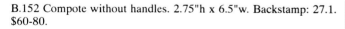

B.152 Compote without handles. 2.75"h x 6.5"w. Backstamp: 27.1. $60-80.

B.154A Top of B.154.

Covered bowls

The key here is being able to reliably distinguish between "bowls with lids" and items more properly thought of as "covered boxes," which are a separate section of this chapter. Although there may be exceptions, the lower portions of covered bowls are much larger than the top portion. They also have sides which curve in two directions, while covered boxes have flat sides (though not necessarily vertical) or sides which, if they curve at all, do so in only one dimension. Covered bowls also must be contrasted with "covered jars." For the most part, "jars" are tall and cylindrical, and in the case of Noritake wares, almost always intended for storing or serving condiments or storing cosmetics. Consequently, various types of "jars" will be found in Chapter C (Condiment Items) and Chapter D (Desk and Dresser Items).

B.157 Covered bowl. 4.25"h x 8.13"w x 6.13"d. Backstamp: 27.0. $110-140.

B.155 Covered bowl. 5.25"h x 9.0"w. Backstamp: 27.1. $110-140.

B.158 Covered bowl. 4.25"h x 8.13"w x 6.13"d. Backstamp: 27.1. $110-130.

B. 156 Covered bowl. 4.25"h x 8.13"w x 6.13"d. Backstamp: 27.0. $120-140.

B.159 Covered bowl. Ducks are 3.5" long. 5.25"h x 7.75"w. Backstamp: 27.1. $340-390.

B.160 Covered bowl. 5.25"h x 7.75"w. Backstamp: 27.1. $340-390.

B.163 Covered bowl. 5.0"h x 5.0"w. Backstamp: 27.1. $180-210.

B.161 Covered bowl. 7.0"h x 7.0"w. Backstamp: 27.1. $90-120.

B.164 Covered bowl. 5.0"h x 5.0"w. Backstamp: 27.0. $150-180.

B.162 Covered bowl. 5.0"h x 6.75"w. Backstamp: 27.0. $250-300.

Nut bowls

Like celery bowls, nut bowls often have handles and could be included in one of the above categories. Because the purpose of such bowls is so clearly indicated by the decoration, they have been clustered into a distinct subgroup within this chapter.

B.165 Nut bowl with six plates. Bowl, 3.25"h x 10.0"w x 7.25"d. Plate, 6.25"dia. Backstamp: 27.0. Set, $120-180.

B.167 Nut bowl. Compare the painting on this bowl to those on the next two bowls. The blanks are the same, complete with the molded in acorns and leaves, but the nuts painted on the surfaces are different. 2.88"h x 7.63"w x 7.13"d. Backstamp: 19.1. $80-100.

B.168 Nut bowl. 2.88"h x 7.63"w x 7.13"d. Backstamp: 27.1. $80-100.

B.169 Nut bowl. 2.88"h x 7.63"w x 7.13"d. Backstamp: 27.1. $80-100.

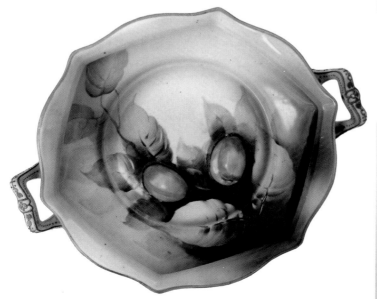

B.166 Nut bowl. 2.13"h x 8.38"w x 6.88"d. Backstamp: 27.0. $80-90.

B.170 Nut bowl set. Individual bowls are 1.5"h x 2.25"w. 4.0"h x 5.5"w. Backstamp: 27.1. Set, $90-130.

Punch bowls

Sometimes, it is obvious that a bowl is a punch bowl. There are some distinct exceptions, however. The modest size of some punch bowls, for example, can prompt one to think of them as "large compotes." Some items that may exemplify this point are included in the punch bowl subgroup of this chapter. It may also occur to some readers that punch bowls ought not be in this chapter at all, but rather should be included in Chapter T, which pertains to beverage items. This is a good point, and had any of the punch bowls here come with cups, I would have placed the entire set in Chapter T. Although puzzling at first, one should remember that the key to Chapter T is, in a sense, cups. Thus, whenever the only item shown is a "bowl" and is referred to as a "punch bowl," I have included it in this subgroup of this chapter.

B.171 Punch bowl. As is often the case, only the footed base has a backstamp. 6.5"h x 12.0"w x 9.0"d. Backstamp: 27.1. $390-450.

B.172 Punch bowl. 5.0"h x 12.25"w x 9.25"d. Backstamp: 27.1. $180-240.

B.173 Punch bowl. Unfooted. 4.75"h x 11.25"w x 9.25"d. Backstamp: 19.1. $160-180.

Salad bowls

Like celery and nut bowls, these bowls usually have motifs and/or supplementary items (e.g., forks and spoons) which make the function obvious. They usually are relatively large compared with other bowls in this chapter, and unlike all other bowls in this chapter, they come (when the set is complete) with a large underplate. Small bowls with small underplates are shown in the chapter on condiment items (Chapter C); small bowls with large underplates are shown in the chapter on plaques, plates, trays, and other bascially flat items (Chapter P).

Boxes

Figural covered boxes

Although "boxes" constitute only a relatively small part of this chapter, it is a particularly important part because, as it happens, some of the most spectacular of all Noritake collectibles are covered boxes such as those shown here. Not all the covered boxes in this book are found in this chapter, however. Photographs of some covered boxes with obvious functions (e.g., the storage of cigarettes) and/or that are just as obviously linked to other chapters have been placed in those chapters (refer to Chapters A and D, especially). In this chapter, covered boxes in the shape of humans or other animals constitute the first of the two subgroups of boxes.

B.174 Salad bowl set. Both spoon and fork have the full backstamp. Spoon and fork, 7.25"l x 1.88"w. Plate, 1.5"h x 10.75"dia. Bowl, 4.25"h x 8.0"w. Backstamp: 27.1. Set, $130-150.

B.175 Salad bowl set. This set was purchased in Australia. The backstamp is one which, although similar to those on pieces found elsewhere, has not previously been recorded in other publications. Thus, this backstamp may have been used only on pieces meant for export to Australia and/or other nearby countries. Plate, 1.5"h x 10.75"dia. Bowl, 4.25"h x 8.0"w. Salad spoon and fork, 7.25"h x 1.88"w. Backstamp: 54.0. Set, $160-190.

B.176 Covered box. 10.38"h x 6.75"w. Backstamp: 27.0. $1700-1900.

B.177 Covered box. 9.5"h x 3.75"w. Backstamp: 27.1. $900-1200.

B.177A Detail of B.177.

B.178 Covered box. Described as a cigarette box in *Collecting Art Deco Ceramics* (Watson and Watson 1993, p. 103), where the piece is shown incorporated into a table lamp. 7.0"h x 5.0"w x 4.0"d. Backstamp: 29.0 (25920). $1900-2100.

B.179 Covered box. Has original price tag: $18.00! 7.0"h x 5.0"w x 4.0"d. Backstamp: 27.0. $1800-2000.

B.180 Covered box. The cat's head (lid) separates from the body just above the red ribbon. 6.25"h x 5.0"w x 3.5"d. Backstamp: 27.1. $800+

B.181 Covered box. 6.5"h x 5.13"w x 2.25"d. Backstamp: 27.1. $400-450.

B.182 Covered box. 6.5"h x 5.13"w x 2.25"d. Backstamp: 27.1. $400-450.

B.183 Covered box. 6.5"h x 5.13"w x 2.25"d. Backstamp: 27.1. $400-450.

Other covered boxes

The other subgroup consists of all the other covered boxes, some of which are in the form of other kinds of living things. In this group are several items that some readers may consider covered "bowls" or "candy dishes." As noted previously, covered bowls have bottoms, much larger than the tops and sides, that generally curve in two directions, while covered boxes have flat sides (though not necessarily vertical) which, if they curve at all, do so usually in only one direction. In this chapter, the last few items do have sides that curve in two directions, but the size of the bottom is virtually the same as the top, thus making it, in the eyes of most collectors, a covered box.

B.185A Top of B.185

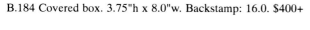

B.184 Covered box. 3.75"h x 8.0"w. Backstamp: 16.0. $400+

B.185 Covered box. 4.25"h x 6.25"w. Backstamp: 27.1. $550-650.

B.186 Covered box. 4.25"h x 6.25"w. Backstamp: 27.1. $140-180

B.187 Covered box. 4.5"h x 6.0"w x 4.5"d. Backstamp: 27.1. $220-280.

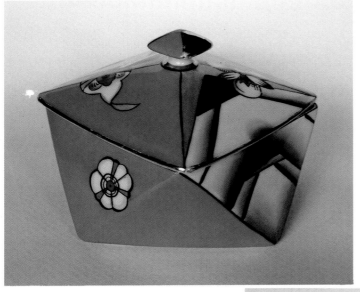

B.190 Covered box. 2.5"h x 5.5"w x 3.88"d. Backstamp: 25.1. $130-180.

B.188 Covered box. 4.5"h x 6.0"w x 4.5"d. Backstamp: 25.1. $220-280.

B.189 Covered box. 3.25"h x 5.13"w x 5.25"d. Backstamp: 25.1. $180-240.

B.193 Covered box. 2.5"h x 4.0"w x 2.88"d. Backstamp: 19.1. $60-80.

B.191 Covered box. 3.75"h x 5.5"w x 4.0"d. Backstamp: 19.1. $60-80.

B.194 Covered box. 4.25"h x 4.13"w. Backstamp: 65.019. $90-120.

B.192 Covered box. 3.0"h x 4.0"w x 2.88"d. Backstamp: 16.0. $60-80.

Condiment Sets and Related Items

Condiments may be defined as edibles normally intended to be eaten *with*, not *as* food. The items in this chapter have a direct link to the serving of such edibles. Below is a list of the subgroups of this chapter. In the paragraphs following the list are comments about the artistic strengths of some pieces and the rationale for the chapter organization. The chapter subgroups are:

Berry sets (pp. 125-127)
Butter dishes (pp. 127-128)
Condiment sets (pp 128-133)
Gravy boat (p. 134)
Honey pots (p. 134)
Jam sets (pp. 135-136)
Mayonnaise and sauce sets (pp. 136-139)
Mustard pots (pp. 139-140)
Oil and vinegar sets (p. 140)
Salt and pepper sets (pp. 140-145)
Swan salt sets (pp. 145-146)
Syrup sets (pp. 146)

Within these subgroups, items are sequenced by size, from large to small. Although height is the simplest and most obvious dimension to use when sequencing items by size, this is often less clearly relevant with condiment items. Consequently, the "height rule" is followed generally but not rigidly in this chapter. In a few instances, the organization may also take into account width and/or certain features of a blank (e.g., tray shape or the presence of ball feet).

One of the more remarkable things about Noritake fancy line items is the attention to design and decorative detail the artists lavished on even the smallest items. Nowhere is this more evident than in this chapter. Many of the items shown here are among the smallest produced by the Noritake Company. If examined closely, however, some of these items are among the most high-quality pieces, pound for pound or gram for gram. The first item pictured (photo C.1) illustrates this as well as any. The design is powerful and the attention to detail (particularly in the beading) is impressive, especially for a mass-produced item.

As impressive as such a piece is, however, most collectors probably would give the "prize" to one of the small figural Noritake salt and pepper sets. For example, refer to the sculptural detailing on the animal figurals (e.g., C.94) and the facial expressions on the figurals in human form (e.g., C.80, C.81, and C.85). Another important subset of the items in this chapter are the types of multipiece condiment sets. For those interested in collecting these items, the big challenge is finding *complete* sets. Two-piece mayonnaise sets (e.g., sets without the spoon) are "a dime a dozen," as the old saying goes. Two-piece honey pots, for some reason, are even more common. If you are one of the many collectors of such pieces, finding a complete set is always a thrill. Even if you do not specialize in this field, and you find a set that is not only complete but also as beautifully designed as those in this chapter, your excitment will last for years.

It was easy to decide that there must be a chapter on condiment sets and related items. The difficult part was deciding what to include and exclude. This is because, not surprisingly, some of the items shown in this book can fit logically into several chapters as they are defined. For example, given the list above and the definition of a "condiment," some readers may have wondered why cream and sugar sets are not listed above (these are found in Chapter T: "Tea Sets and Other Items Related to Beverages"), especially because berry sets are found in this chapter ("berry sets," or "muffineers," are types of tall cream and sugar sets used to hold cream and powdered sugar, which were provided as condiments with berries).

I excluded cream and sugar sets from this chapter for two reasons. First, cream and sugar sets are primarily used when serving coffee and tea. Second, many such sets are parts of tea or coffee sets. This functional relationship seemed to override the fact that cream and sugar can be considered condiments. However, a functional relationship was not always decisive in every situation. Thus, syrup servers are included in this chapter (syrup clearly is a condiment), although they have a reasonably close functional relationship with pancake servers (these are found in Chapter P: "Plaques, Plates, Trays, and Other Basically Flat Items"). Also, some items found in this chapter can, by form alone, be placed elsewhere. For example, butter dishes are similar to pancake servers in that both consist of flat plates covered with domed lids, and on these grounds, could have been placed in Chapter P. Yet butter dishes are included here, rather than in Chapter P because butter is a condiment and pancakes clearly are not.

In this book, the location of some pieces is ultimately a judgment call. Clearly, some items logically could have been placed in several different chapters. My hope is, however, that the choices I have made will make enough sense that the book will be easy to use.

This chapter was an intriguing one to create for other reasons. For example, it sometimes was not entirely clear what purpose was served by the non-salt-and-pepper items in a "condiment set." For those items having small spoons, one may presume that they were sugar bowls, but this conclusion is not without dispute. This issue becomes more complex when it is noted that some of the non-salt-and-pepper items in a set appear to have had no place for a spoon. The usual explanation is that these pieces are mustard pots–a claim for which I would like to see more support.

The backstamps found on the pieces in this chapter are more diverse, as well. In this chapter, many of the backstamps consist simply of the words "Japan" or "Made in Japan." The question then arises as to how one may be certain that a piece marked as such was in fact made by the Noritake Company. The answer, admittedly, is that one cannot be absolutely certain. As previously discussed in the chapter on backstamps (Chapter 3), the collector/dealer may confidently judge that a piece marked "Japan" or "Made in Japan" was produced by the Noritake Company if the color and other details of these backstamps are the same as on number "27" backstamp.

The collector or dealer who doubts this need only examine a complete salt-and-pepper or condiment set which will have the full backstamp on one piece. Usually, the piece with the backstamp will be the largest piece. The most common exceptions are condiment sets in which the underplate is not marked. (When information such as this was available for the pieces in this chapter, it is included as part of the caption.)

It is not only items in some condiment sets whose "true" functions are not known. For example, what were the functions of the swan-shaped items, such as those appearing at the end of this chapter? Sometimes these pieces are described as "mint dishes" or "nut bowls," and the larger swan the "master" nut or mint bowl from which the smaller quantities were temporarily placed in the smaller swans or the "individual mint dishes." Because most people do not consider mints or nuts as "condiments," it could be argued that such pieces belong in another chapter. On the other hand, there are distinct boxed salt sets, consisting of six or eight small swan dishes with little spoons (although these pieces are not shown in this book). Many collectors and dealers believe the large swan bowls were either master salt bowls or used for some other condiment. At the moment, this issue remains unresolved. In light of the known swan salt sets, however, I decided that the swan-shaped items belonged in this chapter.

In summary, this chapter has coherence but this is not to say that there will be no debate about the judgment calls made herein. Even so, I hope that the decisions are understandable overall, and consequently, that the chapter is both informative and easy to use.

C.3 Berry set. Sugar, 7.0"h x 3.0"w. Creamer, 6.0"h x 3.75"w. Backstamp: 27.1. $120-160.

C.1 Berry set. Sugar, 7.0"h x 3.25"w. Creamer, 5.75"h x 4.38"w. Backstamp: 27.1. $150-200.

C.2 Berry set. Sugar, 7.0"h x 3.25"w. Creamer, 5.75"h x 4.38"w. Backstamp: 27.1. $120-160.

C.4 Berry set. Sugar, 7.0"h x 3.0"w. Creamer, 6.0"h x 3.75"w. Backstamp: 27.1. $70-100.

C.5 Berry set. Sugar, 6.5"h x 2.25"w. Creamer, 5.63"h x 3.38"w. Backstamp: 27.1. $70-100.

C.6 Berry set. Sugar, 6.5"h x 2.25"w. Creamer, 5.38"h x 3.38"w. Backstamp: 27.1. $80-100.

C.7 Berry set. Sugar, 6.5"h x 2.25"w. Creamer, 5.63"h x 3.38"w. Backstamp: 27.0. $80-100.

C.8 Berry set. Azalea Larkin #122. Sugar, 6.5"h x 2.63"w. Creamer, 5.63"h x 3.38"w. Backstamp: 29.1 (19322). $130-170.

C.9 Berry set. Sugar, 6.5"h x 2.63"w. $50-75.
Creamer, 5.63"h x 3.38"w. Backstamp:
28.1(Roseara). $50-75.

C.12 Butter dish. 3.0"h x 6.5"w. Backstamp: 27.1. $70-90.

C.13 Butter dish. 3.0"h x 6.5"w. Backstamp: 27.1. $70-90.

C.10 Butter dish. 2.5"h x 6.5"w. Backstamp: 27.1. $90-120.

C.11 Butter dish. Azalea Larkin #132. 3.0"h x
6.5"w. Backstamp: 29.1 (19322). $90-130.

C.14 Butter dish. 3.25"h. x 4.63"w. Backstamp: 27.1. $90-120.

C.15 Condiment set. Oil and Vinegar, 5.88"h. Mustard, 2.25"h x 2.13"dia. Tray, 1.88"h x 11.0"w. Backstamp: 27.1. $180-230.

C.14A Detail of C.14.

C.14B Detail of C.14. Inside butter tray is 3.13" dia.

C.16 Condiment set. Sugar, 4.13" x 4.13"w. Salt and Pepper, 3.75"h x 2.88"w. Tray, 6.5"dia. Backstamp: 27.0. $180-230.

C.17 Condiment set. The tray has no backstamp. 4.5"h x 7.0"w x 2.75"d. Backstamp: 27.1. $180-200.

C.18 Condiment set. The tray has no backstamp; only the bowl has a complete mark. 3.5"h x 7.0"w x 2.75"d. Backstamp: 27.1. $230-280.

C.20 Condiment set. Mustard, 3.13"h x 2.0"w. Salt and Pepper, 2.88"h x 1.88"w. Tray, 1.5"h x 4.88"d. Backstamp: 27.1. $250-300.

C.19 Condiment set. 3.5"h x 7.0"w x 2.75"d. Backstamp: 27.1. $230-280.

C.24 Condiment set. 2.0"h x 5.0"w. Backstamp: 27.1. $90-120.

C.21 Condiment set. The tray has no backstamp. The center item has a removable head but there is no spoon notch; it has full backstamp. Sugar(?), 2.75"h x 2.0"w. Salt and Pepper, 1.88"h x 1.75"w. Tray, 1.0"h x 7.0"w x 2.75"d. Backstamp: 27.1. $220-270.

C.25 Condiment set. 3.5"h x 4.0"w. Backstamp: 27.1. $60-90.

C.22 Condiment set. Sugar, 3.5"h x 3.0"w. Tray, 5.75"w x 3.5"d. Backstamp: 27.0. $110-140.

C.23 Condiment set. The tray has a full backstamp. Large bird, 2.63"h x 2.63"w. Tray, 1.25"h x 7.0"w x 2.63"d. Backstamp: 27.1. $110-140.

C.26 Condiment set. 3.25"h x 7.0"w x 2.88"d. Backstamp: 27.1. $150-170.

C.27 Condiment set. 3.25"h x 7.0"w x 2.88"d. Backstamp: 27.1. $170-220.

C.30 Condiment set. 3.0"h x 5.5"w x 4.75"d. Backstamp: 27.0. $90-120.

C.31 Condiment set. 3.0"h x 5.5"w x 4.75"d. Backstamp: 27.1. $80-100.

C.28 Condiment set. 3.0"h x 5.5"w x 4.75"d. Backstamp: 27.0. $200-250.

C.29 Condiment set. 3.0"h x 5.5"w x 4.75"d. Backstamp: 27.1. $110-130.

C.32 Condiment set. Mustard/sugar, 2.75"h x
2.13"w. Salt and Pepper, 2.75"h x 1.5"w.
Toothpick holder, 1.75"h x 1.25"dia. Tray,
5.25"dia. Backstamp: 27.0. $100-150.

C.34 Condiment set. Backstamp on the salt and pepper is J.1. Sugar,
2.25"h x 3.25"w. Salt and Pepper, 2.0"h x 1.5"w. Tray, 6.0"dia.
Backstamp: 27.1. $180-230.

C.33 Condiment set. Mustard/sugar, 2.5"h x
2.13"w. Salt and Pepper, 2.5"h x 1.5"w. Tray,
4.75"dia. Backstamp: 27.0. $80-100.

C.34A Another view of C.34.

C.35 Condiment set. 2.0"h x 4.0"dia. Backstamp: 27.0. $80-100.

C.37 Condiment set. The tray has no backstamp. The mustard has the full backstamp. The salt and pepper have backstamp J.0. Salt and Pepper, 2.5"h. Tray, 1.5"h x 7.5"w x 2.88"d. Mustard, 3.0"h x 2.0"dia. Backstamp: 27.0. $230-280.

C.35A Close up of C.35, showing decal of Niagra Falls.

C.38 Condiment set. 1.75"h x 3.0"w x 3.0"d. Backstamp: 27.0. $40-60.

C.36 Condiment set. 2.5"h x 4.5"dia. Backstamp: 28.1 (Roseara). $100-150.

C.39 Gravy boat. 3.0"h x 8.5"w. Backstamp: 28.1 (Roseara). $100-150.

C.42 Honey pot. 4.63"h x 4.13"w. Backstamp: 25.1. $150-190.

C.40 Honey pot. 5.13"h x 3.75"w. Backstamp: 27.1. $190-240.

C.43 Honey pot. 3.75"h x 2.75"h x 2.5"d. Backstamp: 27.1. $130-180.

C.41 Honey pot. 4.63"h x 4.13"w. Backstamp: 27.1. $120-150.

C.44 Jam set. Spoon and bowl have full backstamp. 8.0"w x 6.5"d. Bowl, 4.25"h x 5.75"w x 3.5"d. Backstamp: 27.1. $80-100.

C.47 Jam set. 5.0"h x 6.0"w. Backstamp: 27.1. $70-90.

C.45 Jam set. 6.0"h x 6.0"w. Backstamp: 19.1. $90-120.

C.48 Jam set. All pieces except lid have full backstamp. 5.0"h x 5.5"w. Backstamp: 25.1. $90-120.

C.46 Jam sets. 5.13"h x 5.75"w. Backstamp: 27.0. Each, $80-110.

C.49 Jam set. Underplate has no backstamp. 5.5"h x 5.5"w. Backstamp: 27.1. $120-160.

C.50 Jam set. 4.88"h x 4.0"w x 4.0"d. Backstamp: 27.0. $80-100.

C.52 Jam set. 4.5"h x 5.0"w. Backstamp: 27.1. $120-170.

C.53 Mayonnaise set. 5.0"h x 6.0"w. Backstamp: 27.0. $50-70.

C.54 Mayonnaise set. Bowl, 3.25"h x 5.25"w. Underplate, 1.0"h x 6.13"dia. Backstamp: 27.0. $50-70.

C.51 Jam set. 5.0"h x 4.0"w. Backstamp: 27.1. $60-90.

C.55 Mayonnaise set. Bowl, 3.25"h x 5.25"w. Underplate, 1.0"h x 6.13"dia. Backstamp: 27.1. $50-70.

C.58 Mayonnaise set. Bowl, 2.88"h x 4.5"w. Underplate, 0.88"h x 5.38"dia. Backstamp: 27.1. $40-60.

C.56 Mayonnaise set. Bowl, 3.25"h x 5.25"w. Underplate, 1.0"h x 6.13"dia. Backstamp: 27.0. $40-60.

C.57 Mayonnaise set. Bowl, 3.25"h x 5.25"w. Underplate, 1.0"h x 6.13"dia. Backstamp: 27.1. $60-80.

C.59 Sauce set. The underplate has no backstamp. Bowl, 3.25"h x 4.5"w. Underplate, 0.88" x 6.5"dia. Spoon, 5.0"l x 1.75"w. Backstamp: 27.1. $120-150.

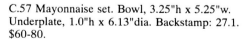

C.60 Sauce set. 3.13"h x 5.88"w. Backstamp: 27.1. $80-100.

C.61 Mayonnaise set. 2.75"h x 5.25"w. Backstamp: 27.1. $60-80.

C.64 Sauce set. 2.5"h x 5.25"w. Backstamp: 27.1. $90-110.

C.62 Mayonnaise set. Bowl, 2.13"h x 5.25"w. Underplate, 6.25"dia. Backstamp: 27.1. $70-90.

C.65 Mayonnaise set. Bowl, 2.5"h x 5.13"w. Underplate, 0.88"h x 6.5"dia. Backstamp: 27.1. $60-80.

C.63 Mayonnaise set. Bowl and spoon have full backstamp. Bowl, 2.13"h x 5.25"w. Underplate, 6.25" dia. Backstamp: 27.1. $70-90.

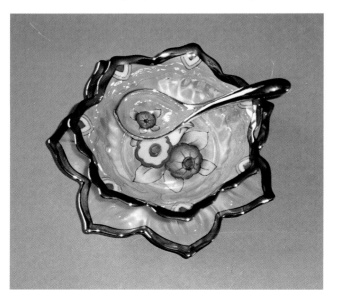

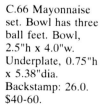

C.66 Mayonnaise set. Bowl has three ball feet. Bowl, 2.5"h x 4.0"w. Underplate, 0.75"h x 5.38"dia. Backstamp: 26.0. $40-60.

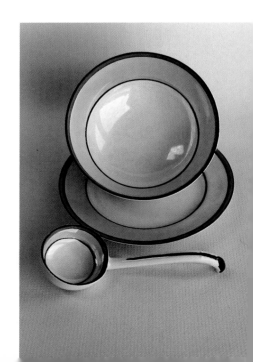

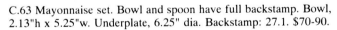

C.67 Mayonnaise set. Bowl, 2.5"h x 4.0"w. Underplate, 5.38"dia. Backstamp: 27.1. $60-90.

C.70 Sauce set. Bowl, 2.75"h x 6.25"w x 4.38"d. Underplate, 0.63"h x 7.25"w x 5.0"d. Backstamp: 27.0. $80-110.

C.68 Mayonnaise set. Bowl, 2.5"h x 4.0"w. Underplate, 5.38"dia. Backstamp: 26.0. $40-60.

C.69 Sauce set. Bowl, 2.75"h x 6.25"w x 4.38"d. Underplate, 0.63"h x 7.25"w x 5.0"d. Backstamp: 27.0. $80-100.

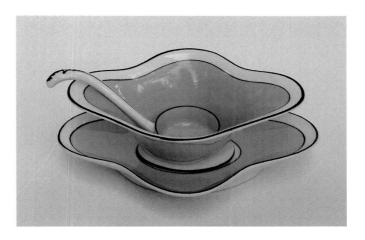

C.71 Sauce set. All the pieces in the black-and-white set (C.70) have the full backstamp; in the blue-and-white set, the underplate is not marked. Bowl, 2.75"h x 6.25"w x 4.38"dia. Plate, 0.63"h x 7.25"w x 5.0"dia. Backstamp: 27.0. Each, $80-110.

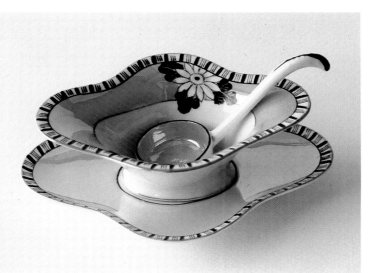

C.72 Mustard pots. Underplates are attached. 3.5"h x 4.0"w x 4.0" d. Backstamp: 27.0. Each, $70-90.

C.73 Mustard pot. 3.13"h x 2.25"w. Backstamp: 27.1. $50-60.

C.76 Salt and pepper set. 4.75"h x 1.75"w. Backstamp: MIJ.1. Each, $70-90.

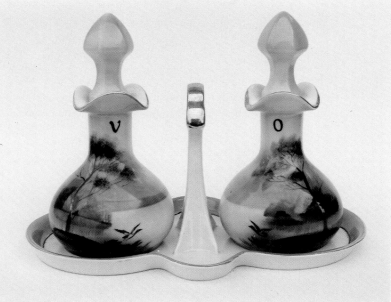

C.74 Oil and Vinegar set. Backstamp: 27.1. $80-100. Bottles, 6.0"h x 3.0"w. Tray, 8.0"w x 4.5"d.

C.77 Salt and pepper set. 3.75"h x 1.75"w. Backstamp: MIJ.0. Each, $70-90.

C.75 Oil and Vinegar set. 3.5"h x 5.88"w. Backstamp: 27.1. $70-90.

C.78 Salt and pepper set. 3.75"h x 1.75"w. Backstamp: J.1. Each, $20-30.

C.79 Salt and pepper set. 3.75"h x 1.88"w x 1.38"d. Backstamp: J.1. Each, $20-30.

C.80 Salt and pepper set. 3.63"h x 1.63"h. Backstamp: J.0. Each, $30-40.

C.81 Salt and pepper set. 3.5"h x 2.0"w. Backstamp: J.1. Each, $40-60.

C.82 Salt and pepper set. 3.5"h x 1.5"w. Backstamp: MIJ.1. Each, $30-40.

C.84 Salt and pepper set. 3.18"h x 1.25"w x 1.25"d. Backstamp: MIJ.0. Each, $20-30.

C.85 Salt and pepper set. Tray has no backstamp. Tray, 4.38"w x 2.63"d. Figure, 3.0"h x 1.88"w. Backstamp: J.1. $120-150.

C.83 Salt and pepper set. Only the basket has a full backstamp; the tray has none. Tray, 4.5"w x 3.25" d. Clown, 3.25"h x 1.63"w. Basket, 2.25"h x 2.25"w. Backstamp: 27.1. $100-140.

C.86 Salt and pepper set. 2.5"h x 1.13"w. Tray, 3.0"w x 2.75"d. Backstamp: 27.1. Set, $150-180.

C.89 Salt and pepper set. 2.75"h x 2.0"w. Backstamp: MIJ.0. $60-90.

C.90 Salt and pepper set. 2.5"h x 4.5"w. Backstamp: 27.0. $60-80.

C.87 Salt and pepper set. 2.75"h x 1.13"w. Backstamp: J.1. Each, $100-130.

C.91 Salt and pepper set. 2.5"h x 4.25"w x Backstamp: 27.0. $90-130.

C.88 Salt and pepper set. 2.75"h x 2.0"w. Backstamp: 27.0. Each, $60-90.

C.92 Salt and pepper set. 2.5"h x 2.25"w. *Left*, Backstamp: 27.0. *Right*, Backstamp: 27.1. Each set, $40-60.

C.95 Salt and pepper set. 2.25"h x 2.25"w. Backstamp: 27.0. Each, $20-30.

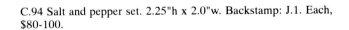

C.93 Salt and pepper set. 2.75"h x 2.0"w. Backstamp: MIJ.0. Each, $10-20.

C.94 Salt and pepper set. 2.25"h x 2.0"w. Backstamp: J.1. Each, $80-100.

C.96 Salt and pepper set. 2.0"h x 1.25"w. Each, $70-90.

C.97 Salt and pepper set. 2.0"h x 1.0"w. Backstamp: MIJ.1. Each, $10-20.

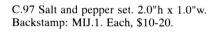

C.98 Salt and pepper set. Tray, 4.38"w x 2.63"d. Salts, 1.0"h.
Backstamp: 27.1. $280-330.

C.101 Swan salt bowl. 4.75"h x 7.5"w x 5.0"d. Backstamp: 27.1.
$150-200.

C.99 Swan salt set. Large, 4.75"h x 7.5"w x 5.0"d. Backstamp: 27.1.
$140-180. Small, 2.5"w x 1.88"d. Backstamp: 27.0. Each, $40-60.

C.100 Swan salt bowl. 4.75"h x 7.5"w x 5.0"d. Backstamp: 27.1.
$140-180.

C.102 Swan salt set. Large, 2.25"h x 6.0"w. Backstamp: 27.1. $140-
180. Small, 1.75" h x 2.5"w x 1.88"d. Backstamp: 27.1. Each, $40-
60.

C.103 Swan salt set. Large, 2.25"h x 6.0"w. Backstamp: 27.1. $140-
180. Small, 1.75"h x 2.5"w x 1.88"d. Backstamp: 27.0. Each, $40-
60.

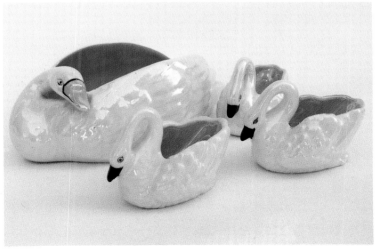

C.104 Swan salt set. Large, 3.0"h x 4.5"w x 3.0"d. Backstamp: 27.1. $100-130. Small, 1.5"h x 2.5"w x 1.5"d. Backstamp: 27.1. Each, $30-50.

C.107 Syrup set. The underplate has no backstamp. Pot, 5.0"h x 5.75"w. Underplate, 5.5" dia. Backstamp: 27.1. $100-130.

C.108 Syrup set. 5.0"h x 5.25"w. Backstamp: 27.0. $60-90.

C.105 Swan salt bowl. 2.25"h x 3.25"w x 2.5"d. Backstamp: 25.1. $70-100.

C.106 Swan salt bowl. 1.63"h x 2.38"w x 1.5"d. Backstamp: 27.0. $30-50.

C.109 Syrup set. 4.5"h x 5.0"w. Backstamp: 27.1. $60-90.

Desk and Dresser Items

In this chapter, for reasons discussed below, there are photographs of items which commonly were used either on or around dressers and desks. Items are arranged in the order indicated:

Within these subgroups, items usually are sequenced by size. I believe it fair to say that the average quality of pieces in this category of Noritake collectibles is judged by a majority of collectors today to be significantly higher than the average quality of pieces in any other chapter. Nearly every piece here is likely to strike the experienced collector or dealer as a strong, desirable piece.

To some, it may seem odd to have desk and dresser items in the same chapter. As with the combinations in the other chapters, there are reasons for this grouping. Although pertinent enough, one of them is entirely an accident of language. The general types of things in this chapter both begin with the letter "D." There is more to the decision to combine these two items than phonological luck, however.

The common bond, with few exceptions, is that these pieces were intended for private (if not intimate) use by women. As such, these items contrast greatly with most of the other items in this book, which clearly were intended for public and social use by both men and women (e.g., smoking items, condiment sets, figurines, lamps, plates, tea sets, vases). Given this fact, it is not coincidental that such a high percentage of these items are so beautifully designed. It appears as if the studio designers and factory artisans knew they could truly lavish their artistic skills and creative efforts on these pieces, given their purpose and audience.

I must include a quick note about the term *dresser doll*. For a time, I resisted using the term, favoring instead terms that gave a more clear-cut indication of the item's function (e.g., powder box). I learned, however, that the Larkin Company (among others) did refer to many of these items as "dresser dolls" and specifically indicated that these pieces had several potential uses (e.g., "for candy, powder-puffs, or trinkets"; p.100 of *Larkin China* by Walter Ayars). I also am aware that there are many people who collect "dresser dolls" as manufactured by many companies. Without any doubt, "dresser dolls" were a "thing" in the past and continue to be such for many collectors.

Even so, not every item that could be called a dresser doll has been so named in this book. As a result, not all of the dresser doll-ish items in this book are found in this chapter. Items in the general character of dresser dolls can be found in Chapter A (where they are termed "cigarette jars"), in Chapter B (where they are termed "covered figural boxes"), and in this chapter (where they are referred to sometimes as "dresser dolls" and at other times as "powder jars").

With the latter instance in mind, one may ask what the difference is between a "powder box" and a "dresser doll." Briefly, the answer hinges on the ratio of the height and width of the lower portion of the "doll." When the bottom half of a dresser doll appears relatively wide compared with its height (that is, when the bottom half looks "short" or "wide" because of this ratio), I am inclined to think of the piece as primarily intended for use as a powder jar or box.

As with many of the opinions expressed in this book, there may well be some readers who will dispute this definitional claim; if so, that is fine. My main objective here is to explain how this book is organized, not to persuade the reader that I am correct in my organizational structure. I hold this view partly because I assume that one of the reader's main objectives is to learn what he or she must know to be able to locate pieces quickly in this book. At other times and places, we may look forward to discussing how these pieces should or could have been grouped.

This noted, I must dicuss those items referred to in this chapter as "talcum powder shakers." The Ayars book provides us a vital bit of information, for in it (e.g., p.101) there are ads for 6" tall "talcum powder shakers" that are in the same shape as some of those shown here. The height of these pieces is important because other similarly shaped pieces, advertised on the same page with their larger "cousins," were items 3.5" tall described for use as salt and pepper shakers. Accordingly, pieces of that size are found in Chapter C, "Condiment Sets and Related Items."

The stated function of some of the pieces in the "Desk Items" section of this chapter also may be unfamiliar to some collectors or open to dispute. In particular, I would note the "calendar holders." Until very recently, I and most other collectors referred to these pieces as "card holders" or more precisely as "business card holders." Thanks to feedback from my good friend Carole Bess White, I am now convinced this is wrong. These items in all likelihood held small, carefully designed pieces of paper which, when properly used, were a perpetual calendar. These pages seldom survived with the original piece, but some examples do exist. For the skeptic, I recommend page 208 of Carole's second book on "Made in Japan" collectibles (see bibliography for details). I also have seen a larger Nippon set of this sort which still holds the paper pages.

Similarly, I suspect there will be debate about the classification of the item listed as a "pen holder." This piece obviously was designed to hold things that were long and thin or other things that would fit within the two-lidded wells or containers at the top of the piece (as we view it in the photograph). One can imagine such sets being used for cosmetic "pencils" of various kinds and the lidded wells for powder or other cosmetics. Just as easily, however, one can see the grooves in front used for pens and the two-lidded sections for pen points and ink (or for paper clips and stamps). Obviously, more information is needed to decide the matter but, whatever the outcome, it seems certain the piece in question was intended for a woman's private use, and as such, it belongs in this chapter.

Finally, a similar point must be made about some of the items in both the "pin trays" and "trinket dishes" subgroups of this chapter. Many collectors may be used to seeing some of these referred to, at shows and in stores, as "ashtrays." As noted in Chapter A, it is almost always the case that ashtrays have an obvious cigarette rest. Therefore, if I did my work with sufficient care, there will be no obvious cigarette rests on any of the items in this chapter. This is not to say that some of these pieces were not used as ashtrays (this may explain some wear patterns that the collector may encounter) nor is it to say that all of these pieces were designed as something other than ashtrays. Instead, it is simply a claim about the decision to include a piece in this or in another chapter of the book. Users of this book are strongly encouraged to check other chapters when attempting to find a particular piece that does not have a completely obvious or singular function.

D.3 For the average person, a photo such as this may seem ordinary enough. Nearly any Noritake collector is likely to view it with amazement, however, for there are few indeed who can do more than dream of the day when they will possess the stunning array of pieces necessary to take such a photograph. All of these pieces are ink wells. The two figurals in the front are 4.0"h x 3.13"w and have backstamp 27.1. Each, $400-450. The two Chinese figures are 4.25"h x 2.63"w and both have backstamp 27.1. Each, $460-520. The inkwell in the center is 4.25"h x 3.5"w with backstamp 27.1. $900+

D.1 Calendar holder. 2.0"h x 5.38"w x 1.75"d. Backstamp: 27.1. $350-400.

D.2 Calendar holder. 2.0"h x 5.38"w x 1.75"d. Backstamp: 27.1. $300-350.

D.3A Another view of an inkwell like the one, *center*, in D.3. The collar base is 2.25"h. This one has backstamp 16.0.

D.4 Ink well. This inkwell is, obviously, the same blank and basic coloring of a piece (*front left*) in D.3. Upon closer inspection, you will see that the decoration on this piece is slightly more elaborate---the only one like this I have seen (so far). 4.0"h x 3.13"w. Backstamp: 27.1. $420-470.

D.3B Another view of the Chinese figural (*left*) in D.3.

D.3C Another view of the Chinese figural (*right*) in D.3. This view of the Chinese figural inkwell shows the interior. The well cavity itself is approximately 1" deep; the bottom piece is 2.25"h overall.

D.5 Ink wells. 4.5"h x 3.25"w. Backstamp: 27.0. Each, $280-340.

D.7A Detail of D.7.

D.7B Detail of D.7.

D.6 Pen holder. 1.5"h x 6.75"w x 6.5"d. Backstamp: 27.1. $250-290.

D.7 Dresser dolls. *Left*, 8.75"h x 3.75"w. Backstamp: 27.1. $1100-1300. *Center*, 9.0"h x 3.5"w. Backstamp: 27.1. $800-1000. *Right*, 8.75"h x 3.75"w. Backstamp: 27.1. $700-900.

D.8 Dresser doll. 6.5"h x 4.0"w. Backstamp:
29.1 (25920). $470-510.

D.9 Dresser doll. 6.25"h x 3.63"w. Backstamp:
29.1 (29312). $750-800.

D.10 Dresser doll. 6.0"h x 3.5"w. Backstamp: 29.1 (25920). $380-430.

D.10A Detail of D.10.

D.19 Dresser set. Tray, 0.63"h x 9.25"w x 6.0"d. Jar, 2.0"h x 3.0"dia. Pin tray, 2.0"h x 2.0"dia. Backstamp: 27.0. $280-350.

D.16 Dresser set. Tray, 0.63"h x 11.63"w x 8.0"d. Powder puff, 3.88"dia. Powder jar, 6.0"h x 4.75"w. Vase, 4.5"h x 1.5"w. Backstamp: 27.0. $550-600.

D.20 Dresser tray. 0.63"h x 10.38"w x 7.0"d. Backstamp: 27.1. $300-350.

D.17 Dresser set. Tray, 0.5"h x 7.88"w x 5.0"d. Powder puff, 3.25"dia. Perfume, 2.5"h x 2.0"w. Backstamp: 27.1. $420-490.

D.18 Dresser set. Tray, 0.5"h x 7.88"w x 5.0"d. Perfume, 2.0"h x 2.5"w. Backstamp: 27.1. $380-450.

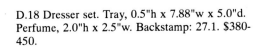

D.21 Dresser tray. 0.5"h x 6.75"dia. Backstamp: 27.1. $280-330.

D.22 Dresser tray. 0.38"h x 8.5"w x 5.75"d. Backstamp: 27.1. $290-340.

D.22A Detail of D.22.

D.21A Detail of D.21.

D.23 Dresser tray. 0.38"h x 8.5"w x 5.75"d. Backstamp: 27.1. $280-330.

D.24 Dresser tray. 0.38"h x 8.5"w x 5.75"d. Backstamp: 27.1. $280-330.

D.24A Detail of D.24.

D.23A Detail of D.23.

D.25 Hat pin holder.
4.75"h x 3.0"w.
Backstamp: 16.0. $50-
70.

D.27 Hat pin holder.
4.13"h x 2.5"w.
Backstamp: 16.0. $50-
70.

D.26 Hat pin holders.
4.75"h x 3.0"w.
Backstamp: 16.2. Each,
$ 40-50.

D.28 Perfume bottle. 6.5"h x 1.88"w x 1.5"d.
Backstamp: 27.1. $500+

D.28A Detail of D.28

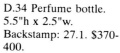

D.31 Perfume bottle.
6.0"h x 1.5" w.
Backstamp: 27.1. $250-
300.

D.32 Perfume bottle.
6.0"h x 1.5"w.
Backstamp: 27.1. $130-
160.

D.34 Perfume bottle.
5.5"h x 2.5"w.
Backstamp: 27.1. $370-
400.

D.29 Perfume bottle.
6.5"h x 1.88"w x 1.5"d.
Backstamp: 27.1. $380-
420.

D.33 Perfume bottle.
6.0"h x 2.5"w.
Backstamp: 27.0. $150-
200.

D.30 Perfume bottle.
6.5"h x 2.5"w.
Backstamp: 27.1. $150-
180.

D.37 Perfume bottle. 5.25"h x 2.25"w.
Backstamp: 27.1. $500+

D.35 Perfume bottle. 5.5"h x 2.5"w. Backstamp:
27.1. $370-400.

D.36 Perfume bottle.
5.5"h x 2.5"w.
Backstamp: 27.1. $340-
380.

D.36A Reverse of D.36.

D.37A Dauber is 3.63" long. Top half of bottle is
2.5" x 1.25". Shown as a half-doll in *The
Collector's Encyclopedia of Half-Dolls* by
Frieda Marion and Norma Werner (Black-and-
white photo MW 631-221).

D.38 Perfume bottle. 3.5"h x 2.5"w. Backstamp: 27.1. $120-160.

D.40 Pin tray. 2.13"h x 4.5"w x 2.63"d. Backstamp: 27.1. $450-480.

D.39 Pin tray. 2.13"h x 4.5"w x 2.63"d. Backstamp: 27.1. $450-480.

D.39A Detail of D.39.

D.42 Pin tray. 2.13"h x 4.5"w x 2.63"d. Backstamp: 27.1. $430-470.

D.41 Pin tray. 2.13"h x 4.5"w x 2.63"d.
Backstamp: 27.1. $430-470.

D.41A Detail of D.41.

D.43 Pin tray. 2.25"h x 2.75"dia. Backstamp: 27.0. $90-140.

D.47 Pin tray. 2.0"h x 4.0"dia. Backstamp: 27.0. $130-180.

D.44 Pin trays. 2.0"h x 2.63"dia. *Left*, Backstamp: 27.0. *Right*, Backstamp: 27.1. Each, $90-110.

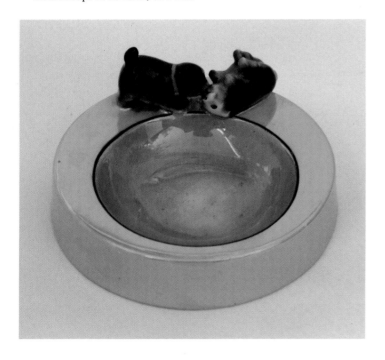

D.45 Pin tray. 1.75"h x 4.0"dia. Backstamp: 27.0. $150-190.

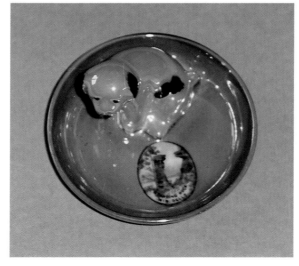

D.48 Pin tray. 1.5"h x 2.5"dia. Backstamp: 16.0. $100-150.

D.46 Pin tray. Standing Rock Wis.[consin] Dells. 1.0"h x 2.75"dia. Backstamp: 27.1. $40-80.

D.49 Pin tray. 3.63"h x 5.63"w. Backstamp: 27.1. $100-120.

D.51 Powder box. 6.5"h x 6.25"w. Backstamp: 27.1. $1300-1600.

D.50 Pin tray. 2.38"h x 2.5"dia. Backstamp: 27.1. $100-120.

D.51A Back view of D.51.

D.53 Powder box. 6.38"h x 4.5"w. Backstamp:
29.1 (29812). $850-950.

D.52 Powder box. 6.5"h x 6.25"w. Backstamp: 29.0 (25920). $1300-1600.

D.53A Detail of D.53.

D.52A Detail of D.52.

D.54 Powder box. 6.25"h x 3.5"d.
Backstamp: 29.1 (25920). $400-450.

D.55 Powder box. 6.25"h x 3.5"w. Backstamp: 27.0. $250-300.

D.56 Powder box. 6.25"h x 3.5"w. Backstamp: 16.0. $200-250.

D.54A Detail of D.54.

D.56A Detail of D.56.

D.57 Powder box. Backstamp has been sanded off; it probably was 27.1. 5.25"h x 5.5"w. $400-450.

D.58 Powder box. 4.75"h x 4.5"w. Backstamp: 29.0 (25920). $900-1000.

D.59 Powder box. 4.5"h x 4.0"w. Backstamp: 29.1 (25920). $420-460.

D.57A Detail of D.57.

D.62 Powder box. 4.0"h x 4.0"w. Backstamp: 27.0. $200-250.

D.60 Powder box. 4.5"h x 4.0"w. Backstamp: 27.1. $400-440.

D.61 Powder box. 7.25"h x 6.0"w. Backstamp: 27.1. $300-350.

D.63 Powder box. 4.0"h x 7.5"w. Backstamp: 19.0. $180-220.

D.64 Powder box. 3.0"h x 4.5"dia. Backstamp:
27.1. $80-100.

D.67 Powder puff
box. 4.25"h x
3.88"w.
Backstamp: 27.1.
$480-530.

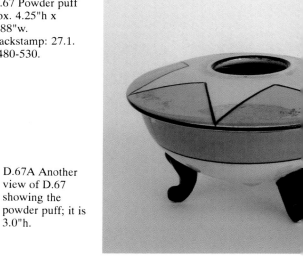

D.67A Another
view of D.67
showing the
powder puff; it is
3.0"h.

D.65 Powder box. Paintings on lids are mirror
images; thus, these boxes are a pair. 2.0"h x
2.5"dia. Backstamp: 16.2. Each, $80-90.

D.66 Powder box. Paintings are mirror images.
2.0"h x 2.5"w. Backstamp: 16.0. Each, $80-90.

D.70 Powder puff box. 3.25"h x 3.63"w. Backstamp: 27.1. $280-340.

D.68 Powder puff box. 4.25"h x 3.88"w. Backstamp: 27.1. $480-530.

D.69 Powder puff box. 3.75"h x 3.88"dia. Backstamp: 27.1. $200-250.

D.71 Powder puff box. 1.25"h x 4.75"dia. Backstamp: 27.1. $180-230.

D.72 Powder puff box. 1.75"h x 4.25"dia. Backstamp: 27.1. $190-240.

D.75 Powder puff box. 1.5"h x 4.0"dia. Backstamp: 27.1. $160-190.

D.73 Powder puff box. 1.75"h x 4.25"dia. Backstamp: 27.1. $180-230.

D.74 Powder puff box. 1.5"h x 4.0"dia. Backstamp: 27.1. $180-230.

D.76 Powder puff box. 1.5"h x 4.0"dia. Backstamp: 27.1. $150-180.

D.80 Powder puff box. 1.0"h x 4.0"dia.
Backstamp: 27.1. $280-320.

D.77 Powder puff box. 1.0"h x 4.0"dia.
Backstamp: 27.1. $440-490.

D.81 Powder puff box. 1.0"h
x 4.0"dia. Backstamp: 27.1.
$220-260.

D.78 Powder puff box. 1.0"h x 4.0"dia.
Backstamp: 27.1. $390-430.

D.82 Powder puff box. 1.0"h x 4.0"dia.
Backstamp: 27.1. $200-250.

D.79 Powder puff box. 1.0"h x 4.0"dia.
Backstamp: 27.1. $390-430.

D.83 Powder puff box. 1.0"h x 4.0"dia.
Backstamp: 27.1. $180-220.

D.86 Powder puff box. 0.75"h x 3.38"dia.
Backstamp: 27.1. $200-250.

D.84 Powder puff box. 1.38"h x 4.0"dia.
Backstamp: 27.1. $130-180.

D.86A Detail of D.86.

D.85 Powder puff box. 1.38"h x 4.0"dia.
Backstamp: 27.1. $160-190.

D.90 Powder puff
box. 0.75"h x
3.38"dia.
Backstamp: 27.1.
$180-220.

D.87 Powder puff box. 0.75"h x 3.38"dia.
Backstamp: 27.1. $220-270.

D.91 Powder puff
box. 0.63"h x
3.25"dia.
Backstamp: 27.1.
$400-440.

D.88 Powder puff box. 1.0"h x 3.38"dia.
Backstamp: 27.1. $160-200.

D.89 Powder puff box. 0.75"h x 3.38"dia.
Backstamp: 27.0. $180-220.

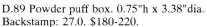

D.92 Powder puff
box. 0.63"h x
3.25"dia.
Backstamp: 27.1.
$160-210.

D.93 Powder puff box. 0.63"h x 3.25"dia.
Backstamp: 27.0. $170-200.

D.94 Powder puff box. 0.63"h x 3.25"dia.
Backstamp: 27.1. $150-180.

D.96 Rouge box.
1.25"h x 2.5"dia.
Backstamp: 27.0.
$100-140.

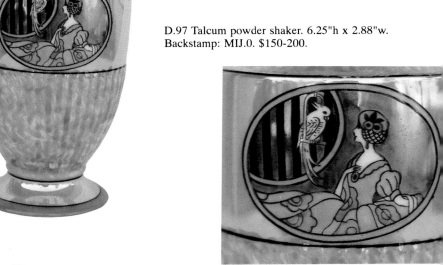

D.97 Talcum powder shaker. 6.25"h x 2.88"w.
Backstamp: MIJ.0. $150-200.

D.97A
Closeup of
D.97.

D.95 Rouge box. 3.75"h x 3.25"w. Backstamp:
27.1. $120-160.

D.98 Talcum powder shaker. 6.25"h x 2.88"w. Backstamp: 27.1. $100-140.

D.101 Talcum powder shaker. 6.0"h x 2.25"w. Backstamp: MIJ.1. $230-260.

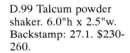

D.99 Talcum powder shaker. 6.0"h x 2.5"w. Backstamp: 27.1. $230-260.

D.100 Talcum powder shaker. This piece has no backstamp. 6.0"h x 2.5"w. $230-260.

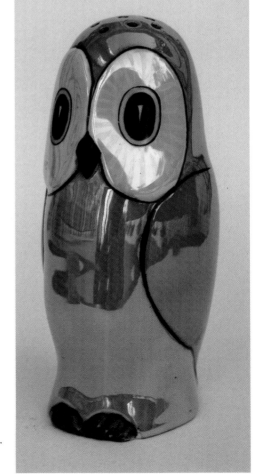

D.102 Talcum powder shaker. 5.5"h x 2.25"w. Backstamp: 27.1. $190-240.

D.103 In July 1996, this photo captured a gathering of all then-known types of heart-shaped trinket boxes. As it happens, these boxes come from four widely scattered collections--- one in the East, one in the North, one in the Far West, and one in the Southwest. The larger ones in the middle row are 1.38"h x 4.13"w x 3.5"d; the one in the center has backstamp 27.1. ($400-480), and the other two have backstamp 28.1. (*Left*, $400-480; *Right*, $300-370). The other four boxes are 1.25"h x 3.63"w x 3.0"d and all of them have backstamp 27.1. (*Upper left*, $350-420; *Upper right*, $300-370; *Lower left*, $350-420; *Lower right*, $350-420). So far, only the box in the upper left has been found with a matching tray (see photo D.104). This suggests there may be other heart-shaped trays out there and can only be good news for the collector! Since this photo was taken, another heart-shaped trinket box has been found, but the photo arrived too late to be included here.

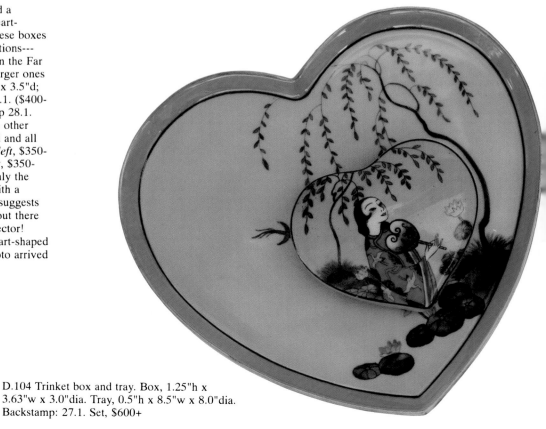

D.104 Trinket box and tray. Box, 1.25"h x 3.63"w x 3.0"dia. Tray, 0.5"h x 8.5"w x 8.0"dia. Backstamp: 27.1. Set, $600+

D.105 Trinket box. 2.25"h x 3.5"w. Backstamp: 27.1. $200-250.

D.108 Trinket dish. 4.0"h x 5.13"w. Backstamp: 27.0. $330-360.

D.106 Trinket dish. 4.5"h x 5.5"w x 4.5"d. Backstamp: 27.0. $290-340.

D.107 Trinket dish. 3.75"h x 6.38"w. Backstamp: 27.1. $290-340.

D.108A Closeup of D.108.

D.109 Trinket dish. 3.5"h x 5.0"dia. Backstamp: 27.1. $430-480.

D.111A Closeup of D.111.

D.110 Trinket dish. 3.5"h x 5.0"dia. Backstamp: 19.2. $330-380.

D.111 Trinket dish. 3.5"h x 4.75"w. Backstamp: 27.1. $250-300.

D.112 Trinket dish. 3.5"h x 4.75"w. Backstamp: 27.0. $250-300.

D.114A Detail of D.114.

D.113 Trinket dish. 3.38"h x 6.5"w x 6.0"d. Backstamp: 27.0. $330-360.

D.114 Trinket dishes. 3.25"h x 7.25"w x 6.5"dia. Backstamp: 27.1. Each, $390-440.

Figurines

In this chapter are photographs of 27 Noritake figurines grouped as follows and sequenced within these groups by size:

Animal figurines (pp. 180-182)
Bird figurines (pp. 182-183)
Fish figurines (p. 184)
Figurines in human form (pp. 184-185)

Many Noritake collectors are unfamiliar with and consequently know little about most of the figurines shown in this chapter. Ironically, the two figurines that are probably best known to most Noritake collectors are the rarest pieces shown in this chapter (F.17 and F.21). Indeed, many would argue that the piece shown in F.17 is one of the most amazing Noritake pieces found in recent years. As for the other figurines shown here, even some experienced Noritake collectors who consult this book may be seeing some of them for the first time. Yet, these are not small pieces that might be missed by Noritake collectors at shows or in shops because of size alone. Rather, in the collector's quest for more gaily colored Noritake items, these mostly plain but very impressive works tend to be missed. In time, I predict many collectors will see this habit as having been a serious mistake.

The reader will notice that some of the captions begin with more than the simple word "figurine." In these instances, the descriptive name is taken from or based on information about these figurines which was made available to me by the Noritake Company. Among other things, this information included the year when the figurines were introduced–a fact of great interest to collectors. It is rare to have information that specifies the exact year in which a Noritake piece was introduced.

Only a few forward-looking collectors have begun to assemble collections of these striking pieces. The photographs in this chapter are from only four collections, two of which are the source of just one photograph each. In other words, this area of Noritake collecting is still referred to as a "young" or "new" field. Although this young field, like most, is underappreciated at the moment, this is certainly soon to change.

F.1 Reindeer figurine. Introduced in 1955. 15.0"h x 9.5"w. Horn span: 6.5". Backstamp: 65.5. $750+

F.4 Deer and fawn figurine. Introduced in 1956. 5.75"h x 7.5"w. Backstamp: 65.5. $250-300.

F.2 Dog and puppy figurine. Introduced in 1960. 6.5"h x 7.13"w x 3.5"d. Backstamp: 65.5. $200-250.

F.5 Figurine. 9.0"h x 6.88"w x 3.88"d. Backstamp: 65.5. $250-300.

F.3 Figurine. 4.88"h x 4.25"w. Backstamp: 65.019. $110-130.

F.6 Mare and foal figurine. Introduced in 1956. 6.75"h x 8.5"w. Backstamp: 65.5. $300-350.

F.8 Figurine. 3.75"h x 4.25"w x 1.25"dia x 1.5"d. Backstamp: 67.019. $120-160.

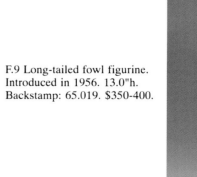

F.9 Long-tailed fowl figurine. Introduced in 1956. 13.0"h. Backstamp: 65.019. $350-400.

F.7 Figurine. 5.13"h x 4.0"w x 2.38"d. Backstamp: 65.5. $80-120.

F.10 Crane figurines. *Left*, crane, introduced in 1954. 10.75"h x 5.25"w. Backstamp: 67.019. $350-400. *Right*, incubating crane, introduced in 1961. 3.5"h x 9.0"w. Backstamp: 78.7. $250-300.

F.11 Bantom figurines. Introduced in 1946. *Male*, 10.75" x 7.63"w. Backstamp: 65.019. $250-300. *Female*, 4.88"h x 5.88"w. Backstamp: 65.019. $100-120.

F.12 Figurine. 10.5"h x 5.5"w. Backstamp: 67.019. $150-200.

F.13 Mandarin duck figurines. Introduced in 1946. *Male*, 5.5"h x 8.0"w. Backstamp: 65.019. $150-200. *Female*, 3.5"h x 6.5"w. Backstamp: 65.019. $130-180.

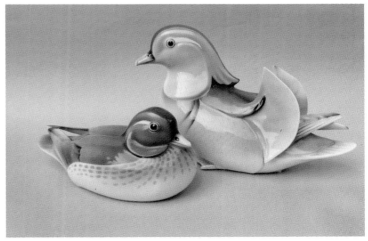

F.14 Azu fish figurines. Introduced in 1953. 2.0"h x 7.75"w.
Backstamp: 67.019. $150-180.

F.17 Figurine.
9.38"h x 5.5"w x
6.0"d. Backstamp:
56.15. $750+

F.15 Goldfish figurines. Introduced in 1953. *Large*, 4.5"h x 8.0"w.
Backstamp: 66.57. $180-220. *Right*, 3.5"h x 5.75"w. Backstamp:
66.57. $120-170. *Left*, 3.5"h x 5.75"w. Backstamp: 66.57. $120-170.

F.16 Figurines. 11.0"h x 3.5"w. Backstamp: 25.1. Each, $380-440.

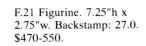

F.20 Drummer figurine. Yagibushi (the drum of Japanese village festivals), introduced in 1961. 7.5"h x 6.75"w. Backstamp: 65.5. $350-400.

F.18 Figurine. 8.88"h x 3.25"w x 2.5"d. Backstamp: 65.5. $200-250.

F.21 Figurine. 7.25"h x 2.75"w. Backstamp: 27.0. $470-550.

F.21A Reverse of F.21.

F.19 Geisha figurine. Introduced in 1960. 8.5"h x 4.5"w. Backstamp: 65.5. $200-250.

Holiday and Special Occasion Items

Over the past 25 years or so, the Noritake Company has produced a variety of items designed both for appeal to collectors and in celebration of important festive occasions in the Western calendar such as Easter, Christmas, Mother's Day, Father's Day, and Valentine's Day. These items, clearly meant for the export market, are made from fine porcelain and produced in limited quantities.

The Easter eggs were the first such limited-edition items. When the series began in 1971, they sold for $10 each and came in fancy, satin-lined presentation boxes (2.38" high x 3.38" wide x 4" deep; see photo H.1). The twenty-fifth such egg was introduced in 1995, and the series is still being produced. These 25 eggs, which are approximately 3" long and 2" wide, are shown in this chapter. They bear backstamp 70.7, just below a large hole (approximately 0.83" dia.) which is closed with a tight-fitting plastic stopper, apparently to allow the eggs to be filled with sand, giving them more mass and greater stability for display.

According to Donahue (pp.60-61), 21,000 copies of the first egg, entitled "Bunnies," were made. In subsequent years, the production run increased slightly. By 1977, however, the number had dropped to 15,000. The selling price had doubled by 1979. Today, these eggs sell for about $75. The secondary market for Easter eggs is somewhat uneven. It is not unusual to see single eggs offered at $25 to $30 apiece. Complete sets, however, are relatively rare and can be expected to be priced accordingly.

The Noritake Company also produced a series of Valentine's Day hearts, one each year for 10 years from 1973 through 1982. Similar to the Easter eggs, each heart came in a presentation box (2" high x 4.25" wide x 3.63" deep; see photo H.2). In the back of these hearts, which are 1.25" thick x 3" wide x 2.5" high, there is a large hole (approximately 0.83" dia.) closed with a tight-fitting plastic stopper, apparently for the same purpose as the Easter egg hole. Backstamp 71.7 can be found on the back as well.

Each year the number of hearts produced varied somewhat. The first year (1973) was an edition of 10,000. By 1978, this number had dropped to 1000, at least according to Donahue (p. 62). Collectors seem to pick and choose among these hearts based on the appeal of the design. Accordingly, one of the more dramatic designs is also one of the most difficult hearts to find– namely the one issued in 1976. All of these hearts are shown in this chapter. In the early 1970s, these hearts sold for approximately $15 new. The secondary market for Valentine's hearts is roughly the same as for Easter eggs; that is, the market is somewhat uneven, although these pieces are generally believed to be harder to find. It is not unusual to see single hearts offered at approximately $40 apiece. Complete sets, however, are relatively rare and can be expected to be priced accordingly.

H.2 1973 Noritake limited edition Valentine's Day heart in presentation box.

H.1 1971 Noritake limited edition Easter egg in presentation box.

Easter
1983

Easter
1981

Easter
1985

Easter
1982

Easter
1984

Easter
1986

Valentine 1978

Valentine 1981

Valentine 1980

Valentine 1979

Valentine 1982

Chapter L

Lamps, Night Lights, and Candleholders

This chapter contains photographs of the following types of items arranged in the order indicated:

The common thread that binds the items in this chapter is *light,* from both candles and incandescent bulbs. For some readers, it will be evident that it is quite reasonable to combine these types of objects. The doubter of this logic may be happier if he or she is reminded that some of the incandescent lamps herein are, in fact, candlesticks wired for the purpose.

Some experts on what I term "candleholders" may wish that I had differentiated between "chambersticks" (which have handles) and "candlesticks" (which do not) at the subgroup level rather than cluster them within a broad group labeled "candleholders." I should note, therefore, that I have used the term *candleholder* precisely because it is broader and more common. Chambersticks and candlesticks are distinguished by the term in the caption and, coincidentally by size, because in this book all the candlesticks are taller than the chambersticks.

The reader will notice that there are only a few lamps and two night lights in this chapter. The Noritake Company certainly produced others, and I plan to include them in future books. In the meantime, I have opted instead for using larger photographs of fewer items. I hope the reader agrees with this decision and my opinion that the two pieces favored by this treatment certainly warrant it.

L.2 Candlesticks. 8.5"h x 5.0"w. Backstamp: 27.0. Each, $100-140.

L.1 Candlesticks. 9.25"h x 4.0"w x 4.0"d.
Backstamp: 27.0. Each, $90-120.

L.3 Candlesticks. 7.5"h x 3.5"w. Backstamp:
27.0. Each, $90-120.

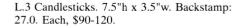

L.4 Candlesticks. 7.5"h x 3.5"w. Backstamp: 27.0. Each, $90-120.

L.7 Candlesticks. 5.5"h x 3.13"w. Backstamp: 27.1. Each, $100-130.

L.5 Candlestick. 5.5"h x 2.5"w. Backstamp: 16.0. $70-90.

L.6 Candlesticks. 5.5"h x 3.13"w. Backstamp: 27.0. Each, $80-100.

L.8 Chamberstick. 6.0"h x 5.5"w. Backstamp: 27.0. $100-130.

L.9 Chamberstick. 4.75"h x 4.5"w. Backstamp: 27.0. $120-140.

L.10 Chamberstick. 4.75"h x 4.5"w. Backstamp: 27.0. $100-130.

L.11 Chamberstick. 3.13"h x 5.0"w. Backstamp: 27.0. $100-120.

L.12 Chamberstick. 3.13"h x 5.0"w. Backstamp: 27.0. $100-120.

L.13 Chamberstick. 3.13"h x 5.0"w. Backstamp: 27.1. $100-120.

L.14 Chamberstick. 3.13"h x 5.0"w. Backstamp: 27.0. $80-100.

L.17 Chambersticks. 2.13"h x 3.25"w. Backstamp: 27.1. Each, $50-60.

L.15 Chambersticks and original box. Tag on box (not visible in photo) says: "10,2035 2 pcs Japan." Box, 2.63"h x 6.88"w x 3.5"d. Chamberstick, 2.13"h x 3.25"w. Backstamp: 27.1. Set, $100-150.

L.16 Chambersticks. 2.13"h x 3.25"w. Backstamp: 27.1. Each, $50-60.

L.18 Lamp. 13.0"h x 8.0"w. Porcelain base, 5.5"h x 5.0"w. Backstamp: 27.0. $150-200.

L.20 Lamp (candlestick). 6.13"h (excluding fixture) x 4.25"w. Backstamp: 27.0. $100-120.

L.19 Lamps (candlesticks). 6.13"h x 4.25"w. With shade, 11.0"h. Backstamp: 27.0. Each with shade, $120-180.

L.21 Night light. 12.5"h x 7.0"w x 6.25"d. Backstamp: 27.0. $2000+

L.22 Night light. 7.75"h x 4.5"w x 3.5"d. Backstamp: 27.0. $900+

L.21A Night light in L.21 illuminated.

L.22A Night light in L.22 illuminated.

Plaques, Plates, Trays, and Other Basically Flat Items

In this chapter, various plaques, plates, serving plates, trays, and other basically flat items have been arranged into the following subgroups:

For the most part, items within these groups are sequenced by size, from large to small. When there are exceptions, these usually are pieces of varying size but the same basic shape and/or similar motif.

Noritake plaques, plates, and trays are what I call "big canvas" Noritake. Here, factory decorators had much bigger and simpler (in terms of shape) surfaces on which to display their talents. The artists' results are evident throughout the chapter, but particularly in the plaques and larger plates on which the famous "lady" motifs can be found. "Lady plates" are among the most sought-after Noritake collectibles. When compared with lady perfume bottles, lady powder puff boxes, and dresser dolls (which are sought eagerly by non-Noritake collectors), there appears to be a slightly greater supply of these plates, although most collectors and dealers still insist that they are quite difficult to find.

The small plates known to collectors and dealers as "lemon plates" are by far more available. Although the term *lemon plate* is generally used for these plates, it is understood that these plates had a variety of uses. The classic image most collectors have for their use is an afternoon tea, with guests offered wedges of lemon neatly arranged on these plates. The plates with loop handles on the side were especially suited for this use, as they easily permitted the host/hostess to present the lemon.

There are approximately 55 lemon plates shown in this chapter. In comparison with other types of Noritake, this is a large number for a single type of piece. Even so, I could have included many more. For the most part, the lemon plates are grouped here in terms of the type of handle or the shape of the plate (round, pointed, or sided). The classic lemon plate has a loop handle on one side of the plate. The other location for the handle is in the center. Some center handles are tall, symmetrical loops; others are solid and shaped roughly like a mushroom.

Collecting lemon plates is a great way to collect Noritake. Except for the rare plates with the lady motif, most of these plates are modestly priced and readily available. More importantly, however, it is with lemon plates that one can quickly and easily get to the point where "collection synergy" can be fully appreciated. Synergy may be described by considering an old saying known to all collectors: "two's a pair, three's a collection." This saying can be interpreted in several ways, but one interpretation in particular is salient here. A pair of lemon plates can be quite striking if they have been carefully selected and well displayed. Almost any three lemon plates, however, even when casually displayed, offer at least as much interest.

P.9 Cake plate. 9.75"w x 9.5"d. Backstamp: 27.1. $60-80.

P.12 Cake plate. 9.75"w x 9.5"d. Backstamp: 27.1. $50-80.

P.10 Cake plate. 9.75"w x 9.5"d. Backstamp: 27.1. $70-90.

P.13 Cake plate. 9.75"w x 9.5"d. Backstamp: 27.1. $70-90.

P.11 Cake plate. 9.75"w x 9.5"d. Backstamp: 27.1. $50-80.

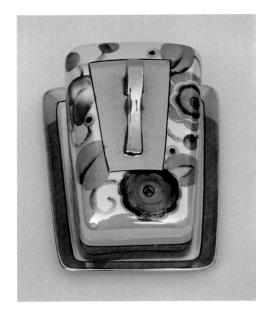

P.17 Cheese server. 4.75"h x 8.0"w x 6"d. Backstamp: 19.1. $80-100.

P.14 Cake set. Cake plate, 8.75"w x 8.75"d. Individual plate, 6.0"w x 6.0"d. Backstamp: 27.1. Set, $150-175.

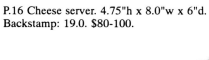

P.18 Cheese server. 3.75"h x 7.5"w x 6.5"d. Backstamp: 27.1. $80-100.

P.15 Cheese server. 4.75"h x 8.0"w x 6"d. Backstamp: 19.1. $80-100.

P.16 Cheese server. 4.75"h x 8.0"w x 6"d. Backstamp: 19.0. $80-100.

P.19 Cheese server. 3.0"h x 6.0"w x 5.25"d. Backstamp: 16.0. $80-100.

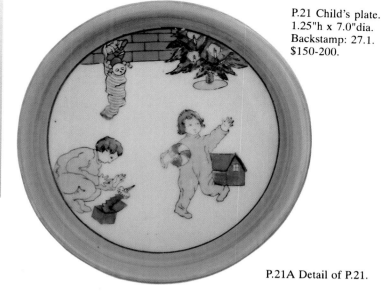

P.21 Child's plate. 1.25"h x 7.0"dia. Backstamp: 27.1. $150-200.

P.21A Detail of P.21.

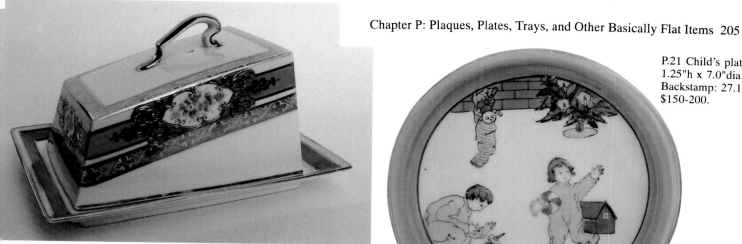

P.20 Child's plate. 7.25"dia. Backstamp: 27.1. $150-200.

P.20A Detail of P.20.

P.22 Child's cup. 2.5"h x 2.5"w. Backstamp: 27.1. $60-80.

P.23 Chip and dip. Plate, 11.5"dia. Bowl, 3.75"h x 6.0"w. Backstamp: 19.1. $90-120.

P.26 Chip and dip. Single piece. 2.5"h x 8.0"dia. Backstamp: 27.0. $60-80.

P.24 Serving plate. Plate, 11.0"dia. Bowl, 4.0"h x 4.5"w. Backstamp: 27.0. $100-140.

P.27 Ice cream set. Tray, 0.75"h x 12.5"w x 7.25"d. Small dish, 5.5"w x 5.5"d. Backstamp: 27.0. Seven pieces, $190-250.

P.25 Serving plate. Two pieces. 4.0"h x 9.0"dia. Backstamp: 27.1. $120-140.

P.28 Lady motif lemon plate. 6.5"dia. Backstamp: 27.0. $200-250.

P.31 Round side-handled lemon plate. 1.5"h x 7.75"dia. Backstamp: 29.1 (39556). $70-100.

P.29 Lady motif lemon plate. Notice that there are no butterflies on this plate. 6.5"dia. Backstamp: 27.0. $200-250.

P.32 Round side-handled lemon plate. 1.5"h x 6.5"dia. Backstamp: 27.1. $40-60.

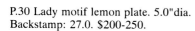

P.30 Lady motif lemon plate. 5.0"dia. Backstamp: 27.0. $200-250.

P.33 Round side-handled lemon plate. 1.5"h x 6.5"dia. Backstamp: 19.2. $30-40.

P.36 Round side-handled lemon plate. 1.5"h x 6.5"dia. Backstamp: 27.1. $40-50.

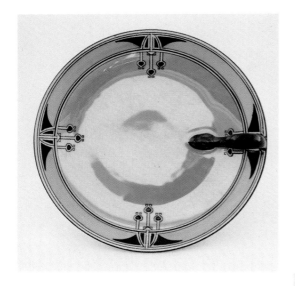

P.34 Round side-handled lemon plate. 1.5"h x 6.5"dia. Backstamp: 27.0. $40-60.

P.37 Round side-handled lemon plate. 1.5"h x 6.25"dia. Backstamp: 27.0. $60-80.

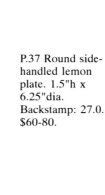

P.35 Round side-handled lemon plate. 1.5"h x 6.5"dia. Backstamp: 27.1. $40-50.

P.38 Round side-handled lemon plate. 1.5"h x 6.25"dia. Backstamp: 27.1. $50-60.

P.41 Round side-handled lemon plate. 1.5"h x 5.5"dia. Backstamp: 27.1. $30-40.

P.42 Round side-handled lemon plate. 1.5"h x 5.5"dia. Backstamp: 27.1. $80-120.

P.39 Round side-handled lemon plate. 1.25"h x 6.25"dia. Backstamp: 25.1. $40-60.

P.40 Round side-handled lemon plate. 1.5"h x 5.75"dia. $30-40.

P.43 Round side-handled lemon plate. 1.5"h x 5.5"dia. Backstamp: 27.1. $40-60.

P.46 Round side-handled lemon plate. 1.5"h x 5.5"dia. Backstamp: 27.1. $30-50.

P.47 Round side-handled lemon plate. 1.5"h x 5.5"dia. Backstamp: 27.1. $30-50.

P.44 Round side-handled lemon plate. 1.5"h x 5.5"dia. Backstamp: 25.1. $30-50.

P.45 Round side-handled lemon plate. 1.5"h x 5.5"dia. Backstamp: 25.1. $30-50.

P.48 Round side-handled lemon plate. 1.5"h x 5.5"dia. Backstamp: 21.1. $40-60.

P.51 Round side-handled lemon plate. 1.5"h x 5.5"dia. Backstamp: 27.1. $30-40.

P.49 Round side-handled lemon plate. 1.5"h x 5.5"dia. Backstamp: 27.1. $30-40.

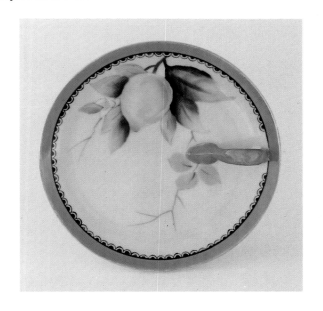

P.52 Round side handled lemon plate. 1.5"h x 5.5"dia. Backstamp: 27.1. $30-40.

P.50 Round side handled lemon plate. 1.5"h x 5.5"dia. Backstamp: 27.1. $30-40.

P.53 Round side-handled lemon plate. 1.5"h x 5.5"dia. Backstamp: 21.1. $30-40.

P.56 Round solid center-handled lemon plate. 1.75"h x 6.5"dia. Backstamp: 27.1. $40-50.

P.57 Round solid center-handled lemon plate. 1.75"h x 6.5"dia. Backstamp: 28.1. $40-60.

P.54 Round side-handled lemon plate. 1.5"h x 5.5"dia. Backstamp: 27.1. $40-60.

P.55 Round side-handled lemon plate. 1.5"h x 5.5"dia. Backstamp: 27.1. $30-50.

P.58 Round solid center-handled lemon plate. 1.75"h x 6.25"dia. Backstamp: 27.1. $30-50.

P.59 Round solid center-handled lemon plate.
1.75"h x 5.63"dia. Backstamp: 25.1. $50-60.

P.62 Round solid center-handled lemon plate.
1.75"h x 5.5"dia. Backstamp: 27.1. $40-60.

P.60 Round solid center-handled lemon plate.
1.75"h x 5.63"dia. Backstamp: 25.1. $30-40.

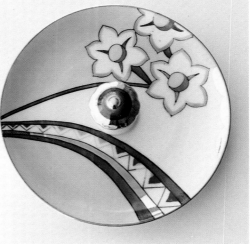

P.61 Round solid center-handled lemon plate.
1.75"h x 5.5"dia. Backstamp: 25.1. $40-60.

P.63 Round solid
center-handled
lemon plate. 1.75"h
x 5.5"dia.
Backstamp: 27.1.
$40-50.

P.64 Round solid center-handled lemon plate.
1.75"h x 5.5"dia. Backstamp: 27.1. $40-50.

P.67 Round loop center-handled lemon plate.
2.75"h x 6.38"dia. Backstamp: 27.1. $20-40.

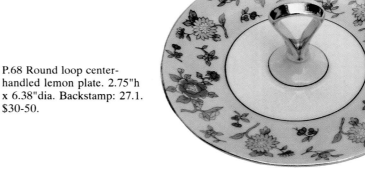

P.68 Round loop center-handled lemon plate. 2.75"h x 6.38"dia. Backstamp: 27.1. $30-50.

P.65 Round solid center-handled lemon plate.
1.75"h x 5.5"dia. Backstamp: 27.1. $40-50.

P.66 Round loop center-handled lemon plate.
2.75"h x 7.88"dia. Backstamp: 21.1. $30-40.

P.69 Round loop center-handled lemon plate.
2.75"h x 6.38"dia. Backstamp: 27.1. $70-90.

P.72 Round loop center-handled lemon plate. 2.5"h x 5.25"dia.
Backstamp: 27.1. $30-40.

P.70 Round loop center-handled lemon plate. 2.5"h x 5.63"dia.
Backstamp: 27.1. $30-40.

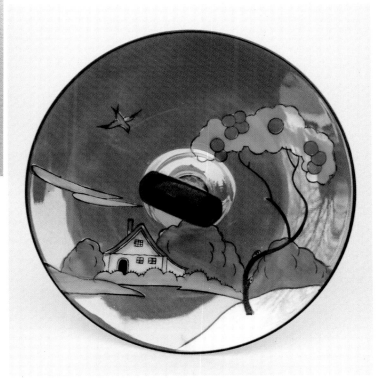

P.71 Round loop center-handled lemon plate. 2.5"h x 5.25"dia.
Backstamp: 27.1. $50-60.

P.73 Sided lemon plate. 2.0"h x 6.0"dia.
Backstamp: 27.1. $30-40.

P.76 Sided lemon plate. 3.38"h x 6.0"dia.
Backstamp: 27.1. $30-40.

P.74 Sided lemon plate. 2.0"h x 6.0"dia.
Backstamp: 27.1. $30-40.

P.75 Sided lemon plate. 3.38"h x 6.0"dia.
Backstamp: 27.1. $40-60.

P.77 Sided lemon plate. 2.25"h x 6.0"dia.
Backstamp: 27.1. $40-60.

P.78 Sided lemon plate. 1.13"h x 5.75"w x 5.5"d. Backstamp: 27.1. $50-80.

P.79 Sided lemon plate. 1.13"h x 5.75"w x 5.5"d. Backstamp: 27.1. $50-80.

P.80 Sided lemon plate. 1.13"h x 5.75"w x 5.5"d. Backstamp: 25.1. $40-60.

P.78A Detail of P.78.

P.81 Sided lemon plate. 1.25"h x 5.75"w x 5.5"d. Backstamp: 27.1. $60-90.

P.82 Sided lemon plate. 1.25"h x 5.75"w x 5.5"d. Backstamp: 27.1. $30-50.

P.84 Pancake server. 4.25"h x 8.88"w. Backstamp: 27.1. $90-110.

P.85 Pancake server. 3.25"h x 8.0"w. Backstamp: 38.1. $50-60.

P.83 Sided lemon plate. 2.25"h x 5.5"dia. Backstamp: 25.1. $50-80.

P.86 Plaque. 10.25"dia. Backstamp: 27.0. $120-180.

P.86A Detail of P.86.

P.87 Plaque. 8.75"dia. Backstamp: 16.0. $350-390.

P.87A Detail of P.87.

P.88 Plaque. 8.63"dia. Backstamp: 27.0. $120-180.

P.90 Plate, round without handles. 8.5"dia. Backstamp: 27.1. $280-320.

P.89 Plate, round without handles. 8.5"dia. Backstamp: 27.1. $300-350.

P.89A Detail of P.89.

P.90A Detail of P.90

P.91 Plate, round without handles. 8.5"dia. Backstamp: 27.1. $300-350.

P.91A Detail of P.91.

P.92 Plate, round without handles. 7.5"dia. Backstamp: 27.0. $280-320.

P.93 Plate, round without handles. 6.25"dia. Backstamp: 27.1. $230-280.

P.92A Detail of P.92.

P.93A Detail of P.93.

P.94 Plate, round without handles. 6.5"dia. Backstamp: 27.0. $130-150.

P.96 Plate, round without handles. 7.5"dia. Backstamp: 16.2. $120-140.

P.97 Plate, round without handles. 7.25"dia. Backstamp: 16.0. $100-120.

P.95 Plate, round without handles. 8.5"dia. Backstamp: 16.2. $80-100.

P.98 Plate, round without handles. 8.63"dia. Backstamp: 27.0. $70-90.

P.100 Plate, round without handles. 7.5"dia. Backstamp: 27.0. $70-90.

P.99 Plate, round without handles. 8.63"dia. Backstamp: 27.0. $80-110.

P.99A Detail of P.99.

P.101 Plate, round without handles. 7.63"dia. Backstamp: 27.1. $40-60.

P.103 Plate with handles. 7.75"w x 7.25"d. Backstamp: 27.0. $30-40.

P.104 Plate with handles. 7.75"w x 7.25"d. Backstamp: 27.1. $40-70.

P.102 Plates with handles. 7.75"w x 7.25"d. Backstamp: 27.1. Each, $40-60.

P.107 Plate with handles. 7.75"w x 7.25"d. Backstamp: 27.0. $60-80.

P.105 Plate with handles. 7.75"w x 7.25"d. Backstamp: 27.1. $30-40.

P.108 Plate with handles. 7.75"w x 7.25"d. Backstamp: 27.0. $60-80.

P.109 Plate with handles. 8.0"w x 4.25"d. Backstamp: 27.1. $40-60.

P.106 Plate with handles. 7.75"w x 7.25"d. Backstamp: 27.0. $30-40.

P.110 Plate with handles. 8.0"w x 4.25"d. Backstamp: 25.1. $20-40.

P.113 Sandwich plate. 3.0"h x 8.5"dia. Backstamp: 19.0. $70-90.

P.111 Sandwich plate. 3.0"h x 10.0"dia. Backstamp: 27.0. $80-100.

P.114 Sandwich plate. 4.0"h x 8.0"dia. Backstamp: 27.1. $300-340.

P.112 Sandwich plate. 4.5"h x 8.75"dia.
Backstamp: 27.0. $100-150.

P.117 Sandwich plate. 2.75"h x 8.0"dia.
Backstamp: 29.1. $70-90.

P.115 Sandwich plate. 3.25"h x 8.0"dia. Backstamp: 27.1. $90-130.

P.117A Detail of P.117.

P.116 Sandwich plate. 3.0"h x 8.0"dia.
Backstamp: 19.2. $70-90.

P.118 Sandwich plate. 3.0"h x 8.25"dia.
Backstamp: 27.1. $80-100.

P.119 Sandwich plate. 3.25"h x 7.75"dia. Backstamp: 27.1. $90-130.

P.122 Serving plate. 2.75"h x 8.0"w. Backstamp: 27.1. $100-150.

P.120 Sandwich plate. 4.5"h x 7.0"dia.
Backstamp: 16.0. $80-120.

P.123 Serving plate. 2.0"h x 7.0"w x 5.75"d. Backstamp: 27.1. $80-100.

P.124 Serving plate. 2.0"h x 7.0"w x 5.75"d. Backstamp: 27.1. $80-100.

P.121 Serving plate. 2.0"h x 8.5"dia. Backstamp: 16.0. $80-100.

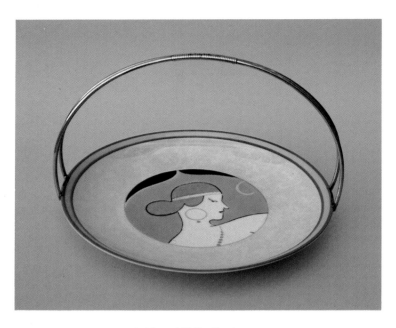

P.125A Detail of P.125.

P.125 Serving plate. 8.5"h x 6.0"dia. Backstamp: 07.0. $200+

P.126 Tray. 14.0"w x 6.5"d. Backstamp: 19.0. $90-120.

P.126A Detail of P.126.

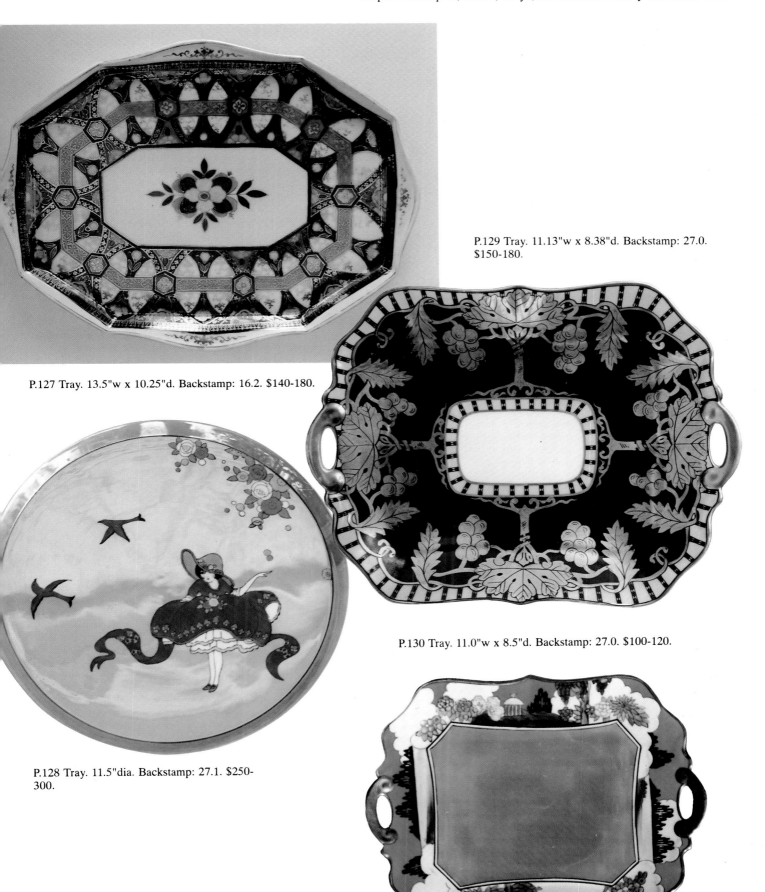

P.127 Tray. 13.5"w x 10.25"d. Backstamp: 16.2. $140-180.

P.129 Tray. 11.13"w x 8.38"d. Backstamp: 27.0. $150-180.

P.128 Tray. 11.5"dia. Backstamp: 27.1. $250-300.

P.130 Tray. 11.0"w x 8.5"d. Backstamp: 27.0. $100-120.

P.131 Tray. 10.75"w x 8.38"d. Backstamp: 27.1. $340-390.

P.132 Tray. 11.0"w x 6.5"d. Backstamp: 27.1. $130-160.

P.131A Detail of P.131.

P.132A Detail of P.132.

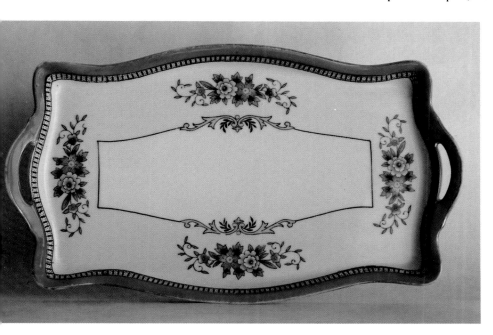

P.133 Tray. 10.75"w x 6.5"d. Backstamp: 28.1 (Roseara). $90-130.

P.134A Detail of P.134.

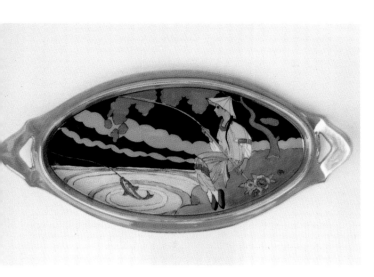

P.134 Tray. 10"w x 5.0"d. Backstamp: 27.1. $280-330.

P.135 Tray. 9.0"w x 9.0"d. Backstamp: 27.0. $340-380.

P.136 Tray. 9.0"w x 9.0"d. Backstamp: 27.1. $340-380.

P.136A Detail of P.136.

P.135A Detail of P.135.

Tea Sets and Other Items Pertaining to Beverages

This chapter contains photographs of tea and coffee sets and other items pertaining to preparing and serving these and other beverages. Within these subgroups, items are sequenced by size, although there are a few exceptions. This diverse but still coherent array of items is presented in the following order:

Children's tea and dinnerware sets (pp. 235-237)
Chocolate pots and sets (pp. 237-238)
Coffee pots, including cafe au lait and
    demitasse sets (pp. 239-241)
Condensed milk containers (p. 241)
Cream and sugar sets and sugar cube holders(pp. 242-247)
Cups, cups and saucers, and snack sets with
    cups (pp. 247-248)
Pitchers (p. 248)
Tea sets and related items (pp. 248-250)
Tea strainer (p. 250)
Tea tiles and trivets (pp. 250-252)

The reader will notice that there are more large photographs in this chapter than in any other. This is partly because these photos are of several pieces, which are often fairly large. Another reason is that many of the sets shown here are rare and exquisitely decorated. This is especially true for some of the children's toy tea sets and dinnerware items. To those unfamiliar with such sets, it may be surprising to see that so much effort was given to their design and decoration. What is even more surprising is to find an undamaged, complete 27-piece child's play set. Although not every piece is shown (to avoid a cluttered photograph), such a set is represented in this chapter.

The term *tea pot* is often used informally as the generic name for pots used to serve hot, mildly stimulating beverages. Even so, the various items covered by this term can and should be distinguished terminologically. Aside from photographs of "tea pots" in this chapter, there are also chocolate pots, coffee pots, and demitasse pots. In general, these items may be distinguished by noting spout length and pot height. Chocolate pots are relatively tall and have short spouts at the top. Coffee pots (both regular and most demitasse sets) are also tall but have much longer spouts that begin near the bottom of the pot. Tea pots tend to be "short and stout" with a spout that usually runs to the height of the pot and often resembles the handle in shape and scale. Although most pots can easily be categorized, the shape and size of some may make this task difficult at times, because the key features appear to border one category and another.

Another definitional issue emerges with reference to "tea tiles and trivets." Is the difference between a tea tile and a trivet great enough to warrant distinguishing them? I must confess to virtual indifference on the matter. I am told, however, that the difference between the two is simple and quite evident. Trivets are completely flat; tea tiles have a tiny rim used to catch a small spill. To the best of my ability, I have followed this principle when I describing the piece in a caption.

T.1 Children's toy tea set. Plate, 4.25"dia. Pot, 3.5"h x 6.5"w. Saucer, 3.75"dia. Backstamp: 27.0. Set of six, $1200+

T.2 Children's toy tea set. Pot, 3.5"h x 5.25"w. Plate, 0.5"h x 4.25"dia. Cup, 1.5"h x 2.75"dia. Saucer, 0.5"h x 3.75"dia. Creamer, 2.0"h x 3.0"w. Sugar, 2.75"h x 3.75"w. Platter, 0.5"h x 7.0"w. Covered casserole, 3.0"h x 6.0"w. Handled serving tray, 0.75"h x 5.5"w. Backstamp: 27.1. Complete 27-piece set, $2000+

T.3 Cream and sugar set. Creamer, 2.25"h x 2.5"w. Sugar, 3.0"h x 3.38"w. Backstamp: 27.2. $100-150.

T.4 Children's cup and saucer. Cup, 1.25"h x 3.0"w x 2.38"dia. Saucer, 3.75"dia. Backstamp: 27.1. $100-150.

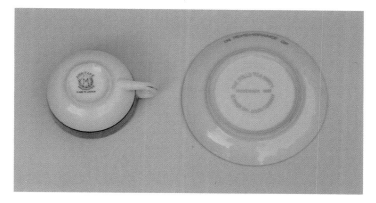

T.4A Underside of T.4. On the underside of the saucer it says: "In remembrance of The Dolls Tea Party November 1927 Denver Dry Goods Company."

T.5 Chocolate set. Pot, 9.0"h x 7.5"w. Saucer, 4.88"dia. Cup, 2.63"h x 3.25"w. Backstamp: 27.1. With six cups, $750-850.

T.6 Chocolate set. Pot, 8.0"h x 7.5"w. Cup and saucer, 3.0"h x 3.0"w x 4.75"dia. Backstamp: 27.0. With six cups, $600-700.

T.7 Chocolate set. Pot, 9.0"h x 7.0"w. Cup, 2.5"h x 3.0"w. Saucer, 4.75"dia. Backstamp: 27.0. Set of six, $550-650.

T.8 Chocolate set. Pot, 8.5"h x 6.75"w. Cup, 2.75"h x 3.0"w. Saucer, 0.5"h x 4.75"w. Backstamp: 27.1. Set of four, $400-500.

T.9 Cafe au lait set. Pot, 6.0"h x 5.5"w. Milk, 5.75"h x 4.5"w. Backstamp: 25.1. $120-180.

T.12 Coffee set. Pot, 6.5"h x 7.75"w. Plate, 8.5"w x 7.5"d. Cup, 2.0"h x 4.0"w x 3.0"d. Backstamp: 27.0. With six cups and plates, $650-750.

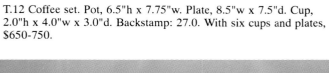

T.10 Coffee set. Pot, 7.38"h x 7.75"w. Cup, 2.25"h x 3.75"w. Saucer, 0.75"h x 5.75"dia. Creamer, 4.5"h x 4.25"w. Sugar, 4.25"h x 3.5"w. Backstamp: 07.3. For set with four cups, $490-540.

T.11 Coffee set. Pot, 7.0"h x 6.75"w. Plate, 7.5"dia. Cup, 2.25"h x 4.0"w. Saucer, 5.0"dia. Creamer, 5.0"h x 3.75"w. Sugar, 6.13"h x 4.75"w. Backstamp: 27.0. With six cups and plates, $650-750.

T.13 Demitasse set. Pot, 7.38"h x 7.25"w x 4.0"d. Cup, 2.0"h x 3.13"w. Saucer, 4.5"dia. Backstamp: 25.1. With six cups, $400-450.

T.15 Demitasse set. Pot, 7.0"h x 6.5"w. Tray, 12"dia. Cup, 2.0"h x 3.0"w. Saucer, 4.25"dia. Sugar, 3.5"h x 5.0"w. Creamer, 2.5"h x 3.5"w. Backstamp: 27.1. Full set with tray and six cups, $550-650.

T.16 Demitasse set. Pot, 6.75"h x 6.5"w. Cup, 2.0"h x 2.75"w. Saucer, 3.75"dia. Creamer, 2.75"h x 3.5"w. Sugar, 3.25"h x 3.75"w. Backstamp: 27.3. Set with six cups, $630-680.

T.14 Demitasse set. Pot, 7.0"h x 7.0"w. Tray, 12"dia. Cup, 2.75"h x 2.25"w. Saucer, 4.25"dia. Sugar, 4.0"h x 5.0"w. Creamer, 3.5"h x 3.75"w. Backstamp: 25.1. Full set with tray and six cups, $550-650.

T.19 Condensed milk container. Underplate, 5.0"dia. Container, 5.25"h x 4.5"w. Backstamp: 27.0. $150-180.

T.17 Demitasse set. Pot, 6.63"h x 7.0"w. Cup, 2.13"h x 2.88"w. Saucer, 0.75"h x 5.0"w. Creamer, 2.88"h x 3.0"w. Sugar, 2.0"h x 3.5"w. Backstamp: 25.1. With six cups, $550-650.

T.19A Underside of container in T.19. The 1.0" diameter hole in bottom makes it possible to push out the can of condensed milk with a finger.

T.18 Condensed milk container. Underplate, 6.25"dia. Container, 5.38"h x 5.5"w. Backstamp: 27.0. $110-140.

T.20 Cream and sugar set. Creamer, 5.0"h x 4.0"w x 3.0"d. Sugar, 5.75"h x 5.0"w x 3.25"dia. Backstamp: 27.0. $200-250.

T.23 Cream and sugar set. 1.5"h x 6.5"w x 5.5"d. Backstamp: 27.0. $90-110

T.21 Cream and sugar set. Creamer, 2.88"h x 4.25"w. Sugar, 3.25"h x 4.88"w. Backstamp: 27.1. $100-150.

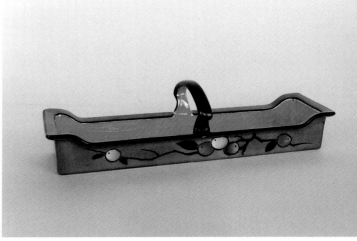

T.24 Sugar cube holder. 2.13"h x 7.25"w x 2.0"d. Backstamp: 27.1. $80-100.

T.22 Cream and sugar set. There is uncertainty regarding the function of this piece. Some collectors believe it was for serving hot butter (e.g., for waffles or pancakes) but others believe the space around the creamer was for sugar cubes. 4.0"h x 6.5"w. Backstamp: 27.1. $100-130.

T.25 Cream and sugar set. 3.88"h x 11.0"w. Backstamp: 27.1. $120-180.

T.26 Cream and sugar set. Creamer, 3.13"h x 4.5"w x 1.63"d. Sugar, 4.0"h x 5.0"w x 2.5"d. Backstamp: 27.1. $80-100.

T.28 Cream and sugar set. Creamer, 3.13"h x 4.5"w x 1.63"d. Sugar, 4.0"h x 5.0"w x 2.5"d. Backstamp: 27.1. $80-100.

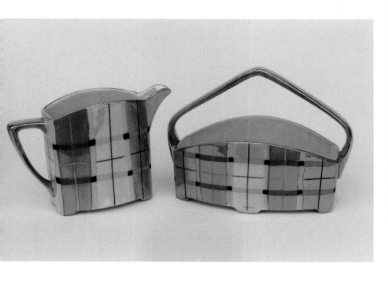

T.27 Cream and sugar set. Creamer, 3.13"h x 4.5"w x 1.63"d. Sugar, 4.0"h x 5.0"w x 2.5"d. Backstamp: 27.1. $80-100.

T.29 Cream and sugar set. Creamer, 3.0"h x 4.5"w x 2.5"d. Sugar, 3.5"h x 4.5"w x 3.0"d. Backstamp: 25.1. $50-70.

T.30 Cream and sugar set. Creamer, 2.5"h x 4.75"w. Sugar, 2.75"h x 4.25"w. Backstamp: 27.1. $40-80.

T.33 Cream and sugar set. Creamer, 3.5"h x 4.25"w. Sugar, 3.0"h x 5.0"w. Backstamp: 27.1. $80-120.

T.31 Cream and sugar set. Creamer, 3.5"h x 4.75"w. Sugar, 3.0"h x 5.5"w. Backstamp: 27.0. $90-130.

T.34 Cream and sugar set. Creamer, 3.5"h x 4.25"w. Sugar, 3.0"h x 5.0"w. Backstamp: 25.1. $80-120.

T.32 Cream and sugar set. Creamer, 3.5"h x 4.75"w. Sugar, 3.0"h x 5.5"w. Backstamp: 27.1. $90-130.

T.35 Cream and sugar set. Creamer, 3.25"h x 4.0"w. Sugar, 2.0"h x 4.5"w. Backstamp: 27.1. $40-60.

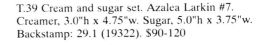

T.38 Cream and sugar set. Creamer, 3.0"h x 5.13"w. Sugar, 4.0"h x 5.88"w. Backstamp: 27.0. $70-100.

T.39 Cream and sugar set. Azalea Larkin #7. Creamer, 3.0"h x 4.75"w. Sugar, 5.0"h x 3.75"w. Backstamp: 29.1 (19322). $90-120

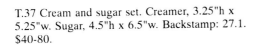

T.36 Cream and sugar set. Creamer, 3.5"h x 4.5"w. Sugar, 5.0"h x 6.0"w. Backstamp: 27.0. $70-90.

T.37 Cream and sugar set. Creamer, 3.25"h x 5.25"w. Sugar, 4.5"h x 6.5"w. Backstamp: 27.1. $40-80.

T.40 Cream and sugar set. Creamer, 3.5"h x 5.75"w x 3.5"d. Sugar, 4.75"h x 6.38"w x 4.38"d. Backstamp: 25.1. $80-100.

T.43 Cream and sugar set. Creamer, 2.75"h x 3.75"w. Sugar, 3.25"h x 4.75"w. Backstamp: 27.0. $30-50.

T.41 Cream and sugar set. Creamer, 3.25"h x 4.0"w. Sugar, 4.0"h x 5.0"w. Backstamp: 27.0. $80-100.

T.44 Cream and sugar set. Creamer, 2.5"h x 5.0"w. Sugar, 3.5"h x 6.5"w. Backstamp: 19.2. $40-60.

T.42 Cream and sugar set. Creamer, 3.0"h x 4.0"w. Sugar, 3.5"h x 5.0"w. Backstamp: 27.1. $80-100.

T.45 Cream and sugar set. Creamer, 2.25"h x 4.5"w. Sugar, 3.5"h x 6.0"w. Backstamp: 27.0. $30-50.

T.46 Cream and sugar set. Creamer, 4.25"h x 5.0"w. Sugar, 4.25"h x 5.0"w. Backstamp: 27.0. $40-80.

T.49 Snack set. Tray, 9.5"w x 6.0"dia. Cup, 2.0"h x 4.0"w x 3.0"d. Backstamp: 27.0. $70-90.

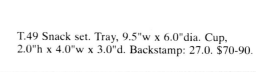

T.47 Cream and sugar set. Creamer, 3.38"h x 4.0"w. Sugar, 2.25"h x 6.0"w. Backstamp: 27.1. $50-90.

T.50 Cup and saucer. Saucer, 5.0"w x 3.4"dia. Cup, 2.0"h x 3.5"w. Backstamp: 25.1. Each, $50-60.

T.48 Snack set. 8.5"w. Tray, 1.0"h x 8.5"w x 7.25"d. Cup, 2.0"h x 4.0"w x 3.0"d. Backstamp: 27.0. $150-190.

T.54 Pitcher. Azalea Larkin #100. 5.75"h x 6.25"w. Backstamp: 29.1 (19322). $200-250.

T.51 Cup (mustache). 2.25"h x 3.75"w. Backstamp: 27.0. $60-80.

T.52 Pitcher. 7.0"h x 7.0"w. Backstamp: 19.0. $70-80.

T.55 Tea set. Pot, 6.75"h x 8.38"w x 4.75"d. Cup, 2.0"h x 4.5"w. Saucer, 5.5"dia. Creamer, 3.75"h x 4.38"w. Sugar, 4.75"h x 5.13"w. Backstamp: 27.1. With six cups, $1200+

T.53 Pitcher. 7.25"h x 6.0"w. Backstamp: 27.1. $80-100.

T.59 Snack set. Tray, 8.75"w x 7.25" d. Cup, 1.75"h x 3.75"w. Backstamp: 27.0. $50-70.

T.56 Tea set. Pot, 5.75"h x 8.0" Cup, 2.0"h x 5.0"w. Saucer, 6.0"dia. Creamer, 3.5"h x 5.0"w. Sugar, 4.0"h x 5.75"w. Backstamp: 16.4. With six plates and six cups, $650-700.

T.60 Tea pot. 2.5"h x 4.0"w. Backstamp: 19.2. $40-50.

T.57 Tea set plate. 7.75"dia. Backstamp: 16.4. $20-40.

T.58 Tea set. Pot, 4.5"h x 9.0"w. Sugar, 3.75"h x 6.0"w. Creamer, 3.75"h x 5.5"w. Backstamp: 27.0. $120-160.

T.61 Tea set. Bowl, 1.0"h x 5.25"w. Plate, 7.5"dia. Cup, 2.0"h x 4.5"w x 3.5"d. Saucer, 5.5"dia. Backstamp: 19.2. For items shown, $40-60.

T.62 Snack set. Tray, 8.75"w x 7.25"d. Cup, 1.75"h x 3.75"w. Backstamp: 27.0. $50-70.

T.63 Tea pot, individual. 4.0"h x 5.13"w. Backstamp: 27.0. $40-80.

T.64 Tea strainer. Only the plate has backstamp. Plate, 4.88"dia. Strainer, 1.0"h x 5.5"w x 3.63"dia. Backstamp: 27.0. $100-130.

T.65 Tea tile. 0.75"h x 6.5"w. Backstamp: 27.0. $80-100.

T.66 Tea tile. 0.5"h x 4.88"w x 4.88"d. Backstamp: 27.0. $60-90.

T.68 Tea tile. 0.5"h x 4.88"w x 4.88"d.
Backstamp: 27.0. $60-90.

T.67 Tea tile. 0.5"h x 4.88"w x 4.88"d. Backstamp: 27.0. $60-90.

T.69 Tea tile. 0.5"h x 4.88"w x 4.88"d.
Backstamp: 27.0. $60-90.

T.70 Tea tile. 0.5"h x 6.0"dia. Backstamp: 27.1. $110-140.

T.73 Trivet. 0.5"h x 6.0"dia. Backstamp: 27.1. $150-180.

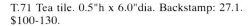

T.71 Tea tile. 0.5"h x 6.0"dia. Backstamp: 27.1. $100-130.

T.74 Trivet. 0.5"h x 6.0"dia. Backstamp: 27.1. $100-130.

T.72 Tea tile 0.5"h x 6.0"dia. Backstamp: 27.0. $80-100.

Vases and Other Items Pertaining to Flowers

This chapter contains photographs of items pertaining to flowers. Within the chapter's subgroups, the photographs are ordered by the size of the piece depicted, from large to small (with a few exceptions explained below). The items are arranged in alphabetically sequenced subgroups as follows:

Although the Noritake Company produced an amazing variety of vases during the time period covered by this book, an adequate sample of these wonderful pieces has never been presented. During my discussions with collectors and dealers from around the country and around the world, it became evident to me that more information about this category of Noritake was needed. Therefore, vases receive special emphasis in this book.

Some may wonder whether it is appropriate to include urns in a chapter on pieces related to flowers. According to *Webster's Dictionary*, urns are "ornamental" vessels, typically with a pedestal or "foot" and a lid. Lids are vital to these pieces, especially because one of the "various purposes" of urns is "preserving the ashes of the dead after cremation." Some dictionaries do state, however, that urns are a kind of "vase;" on this basis, therefore, they have been included in this chapter. Interestingly, most if not all Noritake urns are bolted together where the base and container meet.

Vases comprise the greatest portion of this chapter. In general, the vases are arranged not only by size but also by type of blank. In this book, the largest vase is 12" tall (only one example is shown here). Given what I have seen in collections represented here and in other books on Noritake collectibles, the Noritake Company apparently produced few vases for the export market (after about 1920 or 1925) that were larger than approximately 12". The largest Noritake vase for which I have measurements is 12.75" tall. Unfortunately, a photo of this vase was not available in time to include in this book. This said, it would be prudent to predict, I suppose, that a Noritake-backstamped vase soon will materialize that is taller than this measurement.

In grouping the vases, my general rule was to begin with the largest (as indicated by height and, where pertinent, width). From time to time, however, I have deviated from this rule. In most instances, I am responding to the fact that the Noritake Company sometimes produced vases of the same basic shape in different sizes. Such vases are grouped together, beginning with the largest of the series.

Also, because they are unusual and may have special appeal for many readers, I have elected to open the section on vases with a selection of 19 types of vessels of unusual shape (photos V.20 through V.38). I did this to highlight a subset of pieces which, in contrast to the vast majority of Noritake vases, are asymmetrical and/or have unusually fine or complex features. Although some readers may find these shapes too garish

or bizarre, others will love them all the more for these same qualities. A few of these vases are almost certainly rare but most are not. My aim here has not been to single out a group of rare vases but, rather, to bring to your attention some vases that I thought should not be "lost in the crowd." This should in no way be seen as a suggestion that the other vases in this chapter are mostly ordinary items. Indeed, many of the vases which come afterwards are likely to be thought of by nearly every collector as being more impressive than any of these 19. Even so, and if I may be permitted a personal comment, I find all of these 19 vases to be, without exception, extremely interesting and often quite amazing. Their diversity in both shape and motif will, I hope, both amaze and please you, as it does me.

V.1 Ferner. 3.5"h x 6.5"w. Backstamp: 7.0. $140-180.

V.2 Ferner. 3.75"h x 6.0"w 6.0"d. Backstamp: 27.0. $130-180.

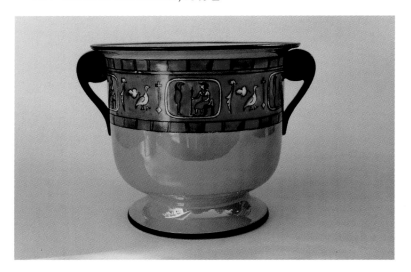

V.3 Ferner. 4.75"h x 6.0"w. Backstamp: 27.0. $160-190.

V.6 Flower Frog. 4.5"h x 3.25"w. Backstamp: 27.0. $140-160.

V.4 Flower Frogs. 3.5"h x 3.0"w. Pink, Backstamp: 27.1. Orange, Backstamp: 27.0. Each, $250-300.

V.5 Flower Frog. 4.5"h x 3.0"w. Backstamp: 27.0. $160-180.

V.7 Flower Frog. 3.75"h x 3.0"w. Backstamp: 27.1. $100-130.

V.11 Potpourri. 4.0"h x 5.0"w. Backstamp: 27.0. $80-100.

V.8 Hanging Planter. 5.0"h x 5.63"w. Backstamp 27.1. $180-200.

V.12 Potpourri. Has no backstamp; the condition of the bottom indicates clearly that it was never marked. 3.25"h x 4.88" w. $60-80.

V.9 Potpourri. 4.0"h x 5.5"w. Backstamp: 27.1. $120-150.

V.10 Potpourri. 8.0"h x 5.5"w. Backstamp: 27.1. $120-150.

V.13 Potpourri. 5.0"h x 5.5"w. Backstamp: 16.0. $70-90.

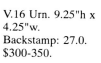

V.16 Urn. 9.25"h x 4.25"w. Backstamp: 27.0. $300-350.

V.14 Urns. Front (*left*) and back (*right*) views. 12.25"h x 6.0" w x 5.13"d. Backstamp: 27.1. Each, $200-250.

V.15 Urn. 9.5"h x 4.25"w. Backstamp: 21.0. $80-120.

V.17 Urn. 8.75"h x 4.5"w. Backstamp: 27.0.
$280-320.

V.17A Detail of V.17.

V.18 Urn. The finial is brass. 8.5"h x 3.88"w.
Backstamp: 27.1. $300-350.

V.19 Urn. 7.25"h x 4.5"w. Backstamp: 16.2.
$120-140.

V.20 Vase. 10.75"h x 5.13"w. Backstamp: 27.1. $270-320.

V.21 Vase. 10.0"h x 5.0"w. Backstamp: 27.0. $200-250.

V.23 Vases. 9.13"h x 3.25"w. Backstamp: 65.019. Each, $80-100.

V.24 Vases. 9.0"h x 3.63"w. Backstamp: 67.019. Each, $70-90.

V.25 Vase. 8.75"h x 3.5"w. Backstamp: 27.1. $350+

V.22 Vase. 9.25"h x 5.25"w. Backstamp: 27.1. $200-250.

V.29 Vase. 7.5"h x 4.0"w.
Backstamp: 29.1. $200-250.

V.26 Vases. These vases are identical, but one has a Cherry Blossom backstamp and the other an M-in-wreath backstamp. 8.0"h x 5.88"w. Backstamp: 21.1 and 19.1. Each, $120-160.

V.27 Vases. 7.88"h x 4.75"w. Backstamp: 27.1 Each, $150-180.

V.30 Vase. 7.0"h x 4.88"w. Backstamp: 27.0. $150-180.

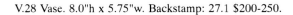

V.28 Vase. 8.0"h x 5.75"w. Backstamp: 27.1 $200-250.

V.31 Vase. 6.75"h x 6.38"w. Backstamp: 77.3.
$70-90.

V.33 Vases. 6.5"h x 3.25"w Backstamp: 27.1. Each, $150-200.

V.33A Detail of V.33.

V.32 Vase. 6.75"h x 5.25"w. Backstamp: 27.0. $90-140.

V.34 Vase. 6.38"h x 6.0"w. Backstamp: 27.1. $110-130.

V.37 Vase. 5.5"h x 4.25"w.
Backstamp: 27.1.
$140-180.

V.35 Vase. 5.5"h x 6.5"w. Backstamp: 27.1. $130-180.

V.38 Vase. 4.75"h x 2.25"w. Backstamp: 27.1. $130-170.

V.36 Vase. 5.5"h x 3.5"w. Backstamp: 19.1. $110-140.

V.41 Vase. 11.13"h x 6.0"w.
Backstamp: 27.0. $200-250.

V.42 Vase. 10.75"h x 8.0"w.
Backstamp: 27.0. $220-250.

V.39 Vase. 12.0"h x 5.75"w. Backstamp: 27.0.
$250-320.

V.40 Vase. 11.13"h x 6.0"w. Backstamp: 27.0.   V.40A Reverse of V.40.
$220-250.

V.43 Vase. 10.5"h x 5.5"w. Backstamp: 27.0.
$160-190.

V.44A Detail of V.44.

V.45 Vase. 9.75"h x 4.5"w. Backstamp: 27.0.
$220-270.

V.44 Vase. 10.0"h x 6.5"w. Backstamp: 27.0.
$150-200.

V.46 Vase. 10.0"h x 6.5"w. Backstamp: 27.1.
$230-280.

V.48 Vases. 10.0"h
x 6.5"w.
Backstamp: 27.1.
Each, $280-330.

V.49 Vase. 9.5"h x 5.5"w.
Backstamp: 27.1. $180-230.

V.47 Vase. 9.75"h x 6.25"w. Backstamp: 27.1.
$190-250.

V.50 Vase. 9.5"h x 5.0"w. Backstamp: 27.0.
$200-250.

V.51 Vase. 9.25"h
x 4.0"w.
Backstamp: 29.1
(29812). $600+

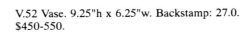

V.52 Vase. 9.25"h x 6.25"w. Backstamp: 27.0.
$450-550.

V.51A Detail of V.51.

V.53 Vase. 9.25"h x 5.0"w. Backstamp: 27.0.
$200-250.

V.54 Vase. 9.25"h x 4.5"w. Backstamp: 27.0. $130-160.

V.57 Vase. 9.0"h x 4.0"w. Backstamp: 27.0. $130-170.

V.58 Vase. 7.0"h x 3.0"w. Backstamp: 27.0. $110-150.

V.55 Vases. 9.25"h x 4.5"w. Backstamp: 27.0 Each, $100-120.

V.56 Vase. 9.0"h x 4.0"w. Backstamp: 19.1. $200-250.

V.60 Vase. 9.0"h x 5.0"w.
Backstamp: 19.1. $90-130.

V.59 Vase. 9.0"h x 6.0"w. Backstamp: 27.0.
$170-200.

V.61 Vase. 8.0"h x 4.25"w. Backstamp: 27.0.
$100-130.

V.59A Reverse of V.59.

V.62 Vases. 9.0"h x 5.0"w. Backstamp: 25.1. Each, $300+

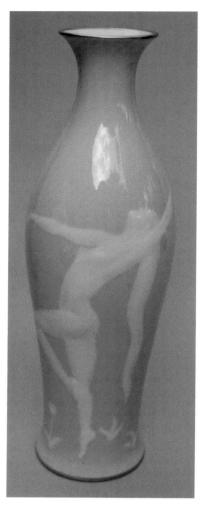

V.65 Vase. 8.75"h x 4.75"w. Backstamp: 29.1 (29812). $1000+

V.66 Vase. 8.75"h x 6.0"w. Backstamp: 27.0. $150-180.

V.63 Vase. 8.5"h x 2.75"w. Backstamp: 33.056. $200+

V.64 Vase. 8.88"h x 5.75"w. Backstamp: 27.0. $130-180.

V.67 Vase. 8.75"h x 4.5"w. Backstamp: 27.0. $130-180.

V.68 Vase. 8.75"h x 5.5"w. Backstamp: 27.0. $180-230.

V.69 Vases. 8.5"h x 5.25"w. Backstamp: 27.0. Each, $150-190.

V.69A Detail of V.69, *Left*. Compare the brush stroke details in this photo with those in V.69B; doing so should make it clear these two vases were entirely handpainted.

V.69B Detail of V.69, *Right*.

V.70 Vases. 8.5"h x 3.0"w. Backstamp: 27.1. Each, $380-430.

V.72 Vase. 8.63"h x 4.13"w. Backstamp: 19.1. $180-230.

V.73 Vase. 8.63"h x 5.13"w. Backstamp: 27.1. $120-150.

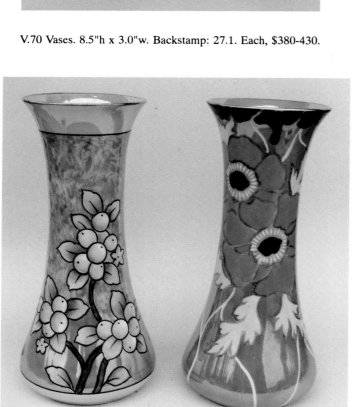

V.71 Vases. 8.63"h x 4.13"w. *Right*, Backstamp: 27.1, *Left*, Backstamp: 27.0. Each, $180-230.

V.74 Vase. 8.5"h x 3.25"w. Backstamp: 19.1. $100-150.

V.77 Vase. 8.5"h x 3.25"w.
Backstamp: 25.1. $80-100.

V.75 Vase. 8.5"h x 6.5"w. Backstamp: 27.0. $160-190.

V.76 Vase. 7.75"h x 5.5"w. Backstamp: 27.0. $150-180.

V.78 Vase. 7.75"h x 3.5"w.
Backstamp: 25.1. $80-100.

V.79 Vase. 8.25"h x 4.0"w.
Backstamp: 27.1. $110-140.

V.80 Vase. 8.25"h x 5.25"w x 3.5"d. Backstamp: 27.1. $170-210.

V.81 Vase. 8.25"h x 5.25"w x 3.5"d. Backstamp: 27.1. $120-160.

V.80A Reverse of V.80.

V.82 Vase. 8.25"h x 3.5"w. Backstamp: 27.0. $220-260.

V.82A Reverse of V.82.

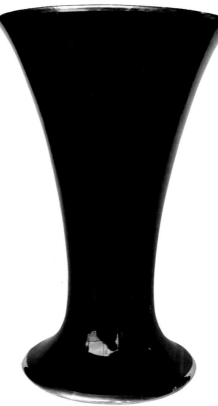

V.85 Vase. 8.0"h x 5.0"w . Backstamp: 27.0. $180-230.

V.83 Vase. 8.13"h x 4.63"w. Backstamp: 27.0. $180-200.

V.86 Vase. 8.0"h x 5.5"w. Backstamp: 27.0. $110-150.

V.84 Vase. 8.0"h x 6.5"w x 5.5"d. Backstamp: 27.0. $150-180.

V.84A Reverse of V.84.

V.87 Vases. 8.0"h x 3.5"w. Backstamp: 27.0.
Each, $100-140.

V.89 Vase. 8.0"h x 5.0"w.
Backstamp: 19.1. $100-140.

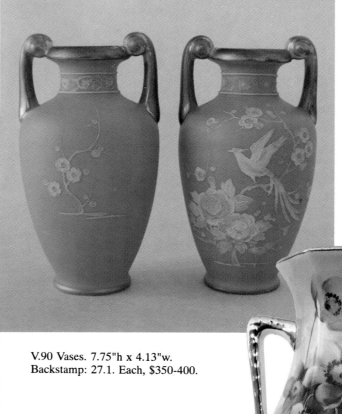

V.90 Vases. 7.75"h x 4.13"w.
Backstamp: 27.1. Each, $350-400.

V.88 Vase. 8.0"h x 5.0"w. Backstamp: 27.0.
$100-140.

V.91 Vase. 7.75"h x 4.5"w. Backstamp: 27.0.
$140-180.

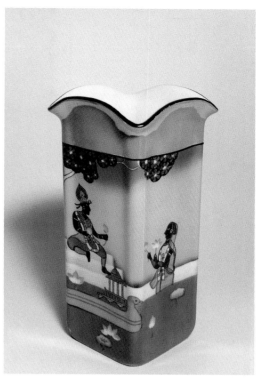

V.92 Vase. 7.63"h x 3.5"w. Backstamp: 27.0. $180-220.

V.94 Vases. 7.5"h x 3.38"w. Backstamp: 29.1 (29812). *Left*, $330-380; *Center*, $330-380; *Right*, $500-600.

V.95 Vase. 7.5"h x 3.38"w. Backstamp: 27.0. $120-150.

V.92A Reverse of V.92.

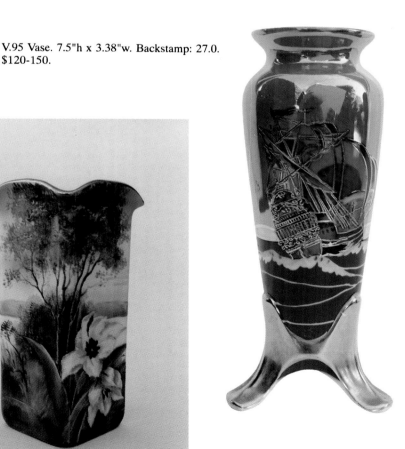

V.93 Vase. 7.63"h x 3.5"w. Backstamp: 27.1. $110-140.

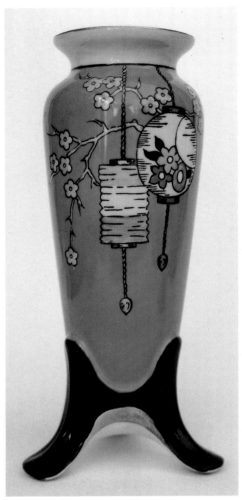

V.96 Vase. 7.5"h x
3.38"w.
Backstamp: 27.0.
$90-130.

V.98 Vase. 7.5"h x 6.25"w. Backstamp: 27.1.
$70-100.

V.99 Vase. 7.25"h x 3.25"w. Backstamp: 19.0.
$100-120.

V.97 Vase. 7.5"h x
5.75"w.
Backstamp: 27.0.
$150-180.

V.100 Vase. 7.0"h
x 4.0"w.
Backstamp: 27.0.
$100-130.

V.104 Vase. 7.0"h x 5.25"w. Backstamp: 29.1.
$120-170.

V.104A Reverse of V.104.

V.101 Vase. 7.0"h x 5.25"w. Backstamp: 27.1.
$120-170.

V.102 Vase. 7.0"h x 5.25"w. Backstamp: 27.1.
$120-170.

V.103 Vases. 7.0"h x 5.25"w. Backstamp: 27.1.
Each, $120-170.

V.107 Vase. 6.88"h x 4.5"w.
x 4.5"d. Backstamp: 27.0.
$80-100.

V.105 Vase. 7.0"h x 4.63"w. Backstamp: 27.0.
$160-190.

V.106 Vase. 5.5"h x 3.75"w. Backstamp: 27.1.
$180-230.

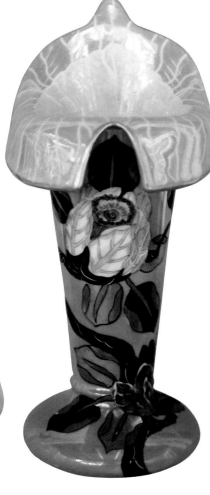

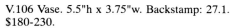

V.108 Vase. This is a large
vase; the height is not a
misprint. 10.5"h x 5.0"w.
Backstamp: 27.1. $240-270.

V.109 Vase. 6.88"h x 3.5"w.
Backstamp: 27.1. $110-160.

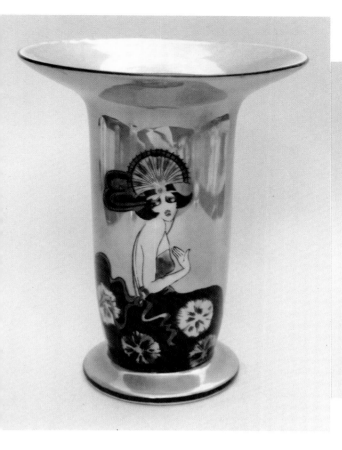

V.113 Vase. 6.5"h
x 4.75"w.
Backstamp: 27.1.
$120-150.

V.110 Vase. 6.75"h x 5.25"w. Backstamp: 29.1
(29812). $400-450.

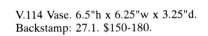

V.114 Vase. 6.5"h x 6.25"w x 3.25"d.
Backstamp: 27.1. $150-180.

V.111 Vase. 6.75"h x 5.5"w. Backstamp: 27.1.
$90-120.

V.112 Vase. 6.5"h x 4.75" w. Backstamp: 27.1.
$230-280.

V.115 Vase. 6.5"h x 6.25"w x 3.25"d.
Backstamp: 27.1. $150-180.

V.119 Vase. 6.5"h x 3.75"w.
Backstamp: 27.1. $140-180.

V.118 Vase. 6.5"h x 4.13"w x 2.75"d.
Backstamp: 29.1. $170-190.

V.116 Vase. 6.5"h x 5.63"w x 3.5"d. Backstamp:
27.1. $250-300.

V.117 Vase. 6.5"h x 4.13"w x 2.75"d.
Backstamp: 27.1. $280-330.

V.120 Vases. 6.5"h x 5.0"w. Backstamp: 16.0. Each, $140-180.

V.123 Vase. 6.13"h x 4.5"w.
Backstamp: 27.0. $120-160.

V.124 Vases. 6.0"h x 6.63"w
x 4.5"d. Backstamp: 27.1.
Each, $120-150.

V.121 Vase. 6.25"h x 4.0"w. Backstamp: 27.0.
$100-130.

V.122 Vase. 6.25"h x 3.5"w. Backstamp: 27.0.
$80-100.

V.128 Vases. *Largest*, 7.25"h x 7.25"w. Backstamp: 76.3. $120-180. *Right*, 6.0"h x 5.5"w. Backstamp: 76.3. $100-120. *Front*, 3.63"h x 3.38"w. Backstamp: 76.3. $60-90.

V.125 Vase. 6.0"h x 6.63"w x 4.5"d. Backstamp: 19.2. $100-120.

V.129 Vases. 6.0"h x 5.5"w.
Backstamp: 27.0. Each, $130-180.

V.126 Vase. 6.0"h x 3.5"w. Backstamp: 27.1.
$100-140.

V.127 Vase. 6.0"h x 3.5"w. Backstamp: 27.1.
$100-140.

V.133 Vase. 6.0"h x 5.0"w x 3.5"d. Backstamp: 27.0. $150-200.

V.130 Vase. 6.0"h x 4.0"w. Backstamp: 27.0. $120-160.

V.134 Vase. 6.0"h x 5.0"w x 3.5"d. Backstamp: 27.1. $100-120.

V.131 Vases. 6.0"h x 4.0"w. *Left*, Backstamp: 25.1. *Right*, Backstamp: 27.1. Each, $100-130.

V.132 Vase. Azalea Larkin # 187. 5.5"h x 4.0"w. Backstamp: 29.1 (19322). $190-250.

V.137 Vase. 5.88"h x 6.75"w. Backstamp: 27.1. $130-180.

V.137A Top view of V.137.

V.135 Vase. 6.0"h x 2.63"w. Backstamp: 27.0. $70-90.

V.136 Vase. 6.0"h x 3.0"w. Backstamp: 27.1. $80-100.

V.138 Vase. 5.75"h x 3.63"w. Backstamp: 16.2. $110-150.

V.141 Vase. 5.75"h
x 5.25"w. x 2.0"d.
Backstamp: 27.1.
$80-100.

V.139 Vase. 5.63"h x 3.25"w. Backstamp: 27.0.
$120-180.

V.140 Vase. 5.75"h x 4.0" w. Backstamp: 27.0.
$90-120.

V.142 Vase. 5.75"h
x 4.13"w.
Backstamp: 27.1.
$90-130.

V.143 Vase. 5.75"h x 4.13"w. Backstamp: 28.1
(Roseara). $110-140.

V.146 Vase. 5.25"h x 7.5"w. Backstamp: 27.1. $130-180.

V.144 Vase. 5.5"h x 4.0"w. Backstamp: 27.1.
$120-150.

V.146A Reverse of V.146.

V.147 Vase. 5.25"h x 7.5"w. Backstamp: 27.1. $160-210.

V.145 Vase. 5.5"h x 4.5"w. Backstamp: 27.1. $70-100.

V.150 Vase. 5.0"h x 3.5"w. Backstamp: 27.1. $110-140.

V.148 Vase. 5.0"h x 4.0"w. Backstamp: 27.0. $70-90.

V.150A Detail of V.150.

V.148A Detail of V.148.

V.149 Vase. Rare color. 5.0"h x 4.5"w. Backstamp: 27.1. $150-180.

V.153 Vase. 5.0"h x 3.0"w x 2.75"d. Backstamp: 19.0. $140-170.

V.151 Vase. 5.13"h x 3.5"w x 3.0"d. Backstamp: 27.1. $150-170.

V.154 Vase. 5.0"h x 3.0"w x 2.75"d. Backstamp: 27.0. $130-160.

V.152 Vase. 5.13"h x 3.5"w x 3.0"d. Bird, 2.25"h. Backstamp: 27.0. $100-130.

V.155 Vase. 5.0"h x 3.0"w x 2.75"d. Backstamp: 27.1. $130-160.

V.156 Vase. 5.0"h x 2.5"w. Backstamp: 16.0. $70-100.

V.157 Vase. 5.0"h x 3.25"w. Backstamp: 16.2. $70-100.

V.159 Vase. 4.75"h x 2.38"w. Backstamp: 27.1. $60-80.

V.158 Vase. 5.0"h x 3.13"w. Backstamp: 16.0. $70-100.

V.160 Vases. Arranged to show front and back. 4.5"h x 4.0"w. Backstamp: 15.01 (44047). Each, $70-90.

V.163 Vase. 4.25"h x 2.5"w.
Backstamp: 27.0. $80-100.

V.161 Vase. 4.5"h x 2.25"w. Backstamp: 27.1.
$50-70.

V.162 Vase. 4.38"h x 3.5"w. Backstamp: 16.2.
$50-70.

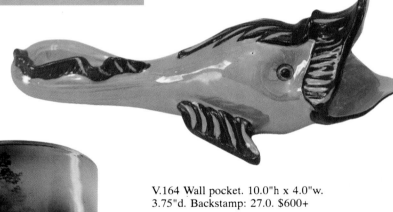

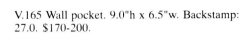

V.164 Wall pocket. 10.0"h x 4.0"w.
3.75"d. Backstamp: 27.0. $600+

V.165 Wall pocket. 9.0"h x 6.5"w. Backstamp:
27.0. $170-200.

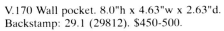

V.168 Wall pocket. 8.25"h x 4.0"w. Backstamp: 27.1. $900+

V.169 Wall pocket. 7.5"h x 4.75"w. Backstamp: 16.0. $900+

V.166 Wall pocket. 8.75"h x 4.0"w x 3.0"d. Backstamp: 27.1. $180-230.

V.167 Wall pocket. 8.5"h x 6.63"w. Backstamp: 27.1. $250-300.

V.170A Detail of V170.

V.170 Wall pocket. 8.0"h x 4.63"w x 2.63"d. Backstamp: 29.1 (29812). $450-500.

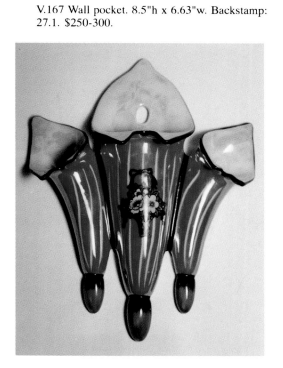

V.173 Wall pocket. 9.25"h x 4.63"w x 2.63"d. Backstamp: 27.0. $190-240.

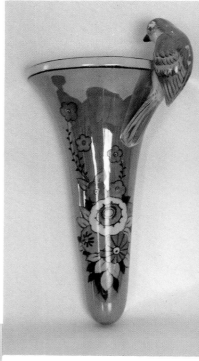

V.171 Wall pocket. 8.0"h x 4.63"w x 2.63"d. Backstamp: 29.1 (29812). $430-520.

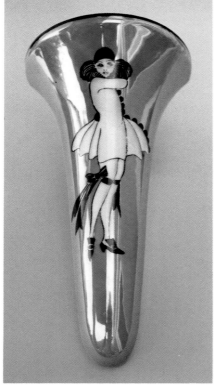

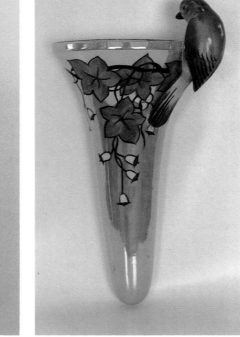

V.174 Wall pocket. 8.25"h x 4.63"w x 2.63"d. Backstamp: 27.0. $160-190.

V.172 Wall pocket. 8.0"h x 4.63"w x 2.63"d. Backstamp: 29.1. $440-480.

V.175 Wall pocket. 8.25"h x 4.63"w x 2.63"d. Backstamp: 27.0. $150-180.

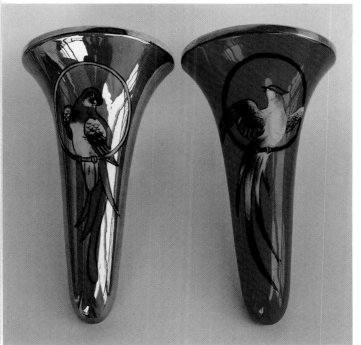

V.178 Wall pocket.
8.0"h x 4.63"w x
2.63"d. Backstamp:
29.1. $150-180.

V.176 Wall pocket. 9.25"h x 4.38"w x 2.25"d.
Backstamp: 27.1. $110-140.

V.177 Wall pocket. 8.0"h x 4.63"w x 2.63"d.
Backstamp: 19.2. $140-170.

V.180 Wall pocket.
8.0"h x 4.63"w x
2.63"d. Backstamp:
27.0. $130-150.

V.179 Wall pockets. 8.0"h x 4.63"w x 2.63"d. Backstamp: 27.1.
Each, $150-180.

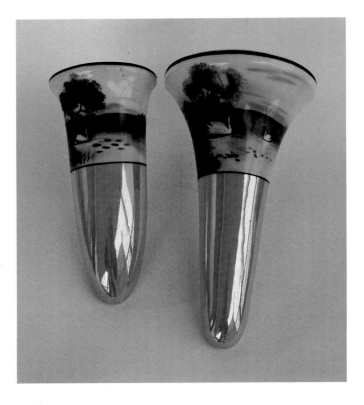

V.181 Wall pockets. *Left*, 7.0"h x 3.25"w x 1.75"d. Backstamp: 27.1. $70-90. *Right*, 8.0"h x 4.5"w x 2.63"d. Backstamp: 27.1. $120-140.

V.184 Wall pocket. 8.0"h x 2.25"w 2.0"d. Backstamp: 27.1. $330-380.

V.185 Wall pocket. 8.25"h x 2.25"w. Backstamp: 27.1. $120-150.

V.182 Wall pockets. 6.0"h x 2.88"w. *Left*, no backstamp. *Right*, Backstamp: 27.1. Each, $70-90.

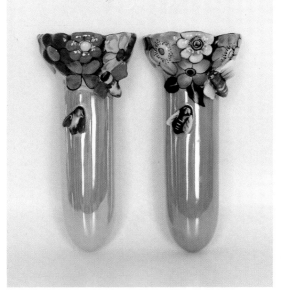

V.183 Wall pockets. 5.25"h. *Right*, Backstamp: 27.1. *Left*, Backstamp: 27.0. Each, $90-120.

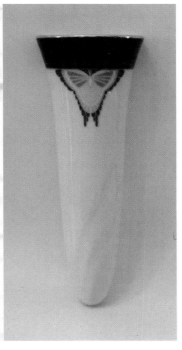

V.189 Vase. 6.63"h x
5.0"w x 2.0"d.
Backstamp: 27.0. $170-
200.

V.186 Wall pocket.
8.25"h 2.25"w.
Backstamp: 27.1. $110-
140.

V.188 Wall pocket.
6.63"h x 5.0"w x 2.0"d.
Backstamp: 27.0. $420-
460.

V.187 Wall pocket.
7.25"h x 2.88"w.
Backstamp: 86.5. $60-
80.

V.190 Wall pocket. 6.63"h x 5.0"w x 2.0"d.
Backstamp: 27.1. $170-200.

V.191 Wall pocket.
7.0"h x 3.5"w.
Backstamp: 27.1.
$160-190.

V.194 Wall pocket.
8.0"h x 5.63"w.
Backstamp: 27.1.
$150-180.

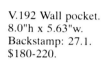

V.192 Wall pocket.
8.0"h x 5.63"w.
Backstamp: 27.1.
$180-220.

V.195 Wall pocket. 5.5"h x 7.75"w. Backstamp: 27.0. $350-400.

V.196 Wall pocket. 5.5"h x 7.75"w. Backstamp: 27.0. $330-380.

V.193 Wall pocket.
8.0"h x 5.63"w.
Backstamp: 27.1.
$170-190.

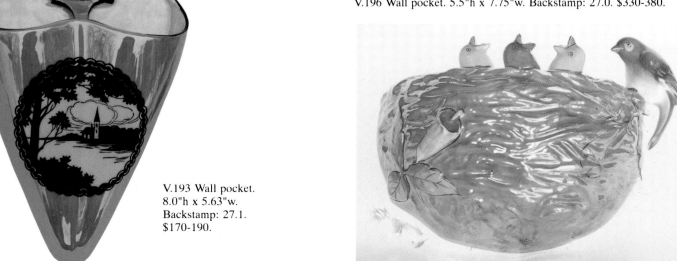

Miscellaneous Items

This chapter contains photographs of the following miscellaneous Noritake collectible items as indicated:

One way to remember the rationale for the organization of this chapter, at least for those who can bear bad puns, is to note that I have saved "Z best for last." Well, if not "Z" absolute best, then certainly some among "Z" very best that this book and "Z" Noritake Company has to offer (I promise I won't do it again).

Initially, I had hoped it would be possible to do this book without including a "miscellaneous" chapter and, of course, I could have avoided it in several ways. For example, I could have easily created several very small chapters. I also could have forced the items in this chapter into other existing chapters. For example, I could have wedged the bell, egg cups, place card holders, napkin rings, toast racks, spooners, and toothpick holders into Chapter T, arguing that these items could be used when serving coffee or tea. Or, I could have placed the incense burner and shaving mug in Chapter D. Instead, for what I hope are fairly good reasons, I have chosen to place these and other distinctive items into this chapter.

Up to now, in this book, I have tried to avoid commenting on particularly rare items, although I admit to having been unable to resist discussion on several pieces, such as the Gemini and Sisters "super bowls," a few of the unusual vases, and some of the amazing tea sets, to name a few. Once more, I beg your indulgence, for I simply cannot resist commenting about one item in this chapter, which is the "painting on porcelain."

The photograph of this piece perfectly captures the vivid red that dominates the painting. Much of the strength of this piece is a product of this awesome color, so it is important that you are able to gain some sense of it through this photograph. In a booklet provided by the Noritake Company and in Lou Ann Donahue's book (p.54), there are a few comments about this distinctive red glaze that I wish to share with you.

By name, this fiery red color is known as *Shinsha glaze*. Although described in the Noritake booklet as "one of the most beautiful [art forms] perfected by the craftsmen of Noritake," it is a technique that was developed more than 600 years ago. When it was first developed, the color was said to be so brilliant, it was presumed the artist used "powder from ground rubies" as its foundation. Another story links this color and the blood sacrifice artists would make if the red color of a piece did not match their expectations. Even now, the color is sometimes referred to as the "red of sacrifice."

When I saw the piece (shown in photo Z.8), I was struck by the contrast between the depth and power of the color and the soft, gentle character of the painting's subject matter. Over the years, I have found that I can tell when I am going to "splurge" on a piece. It is when I *cannot* stop looking at it. This is a piece that "has me in its spell." The painting on porcelain is such a piece. If, from the photo in this chapter, the piece does not "grab you" or "hold you in its spell," blame it on the photo; I assure you, this piece is absolutely breathtaking, should you see it "in the flesh." It is truly a remarkable work of art.

Z.1 Bell. 3.75"h x 3.0"w. Backstamp: 27.1. $100-140

Z.2 Biscuit jar. 6.75"h x 5.5"w. Backstamp: 27.0. $180-200.

Z.3 Biscuit jar. 8.5"h x 6.5"w. Backstamp: 16.2. $180-200.

Z.6 Egg set. 2.63"h x 4.25"w x 2.75"d. Backstamp: 27.0. $40-70.

Z.7 Incense burner. 6.5"h x 5.0"w. Backstamp: 27.0. $550+

Z.7A Detail of Z.7.

Z.4 Egg cups. Azalea Larkin #120. 3.0"h x 2.25"w. Backstamp: 29.1 (19322). Each, $60-80.

Z.5 Egg set. 2.25"h x 4.25"w. Backstamp: 27.1. $60-90.

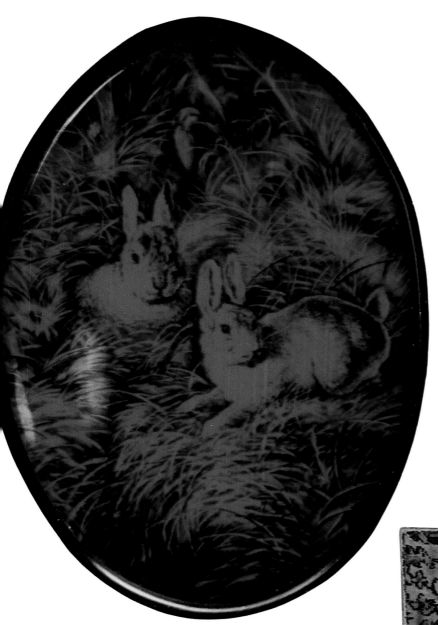

Z.10 Place card holders. 1.5"h x 1.25"w. Backstamp: 27.1. Each, $20-30.

Z.8 Painting on porcelain. Although not visible in the photo, this extremely rare piece is dated and appears to be signed under the glaze, approximately halfway between the rabbit on the right and the bottom edge of the piece. Only the first letter of the apparent signature, an "M," can be made out clearly; the other letter-like marks look approximately like "lijrh." The date, however, is clear: 1946 10.27 (i.e., October 27, 1946). 9.25"h x 6.63"w. Backstamp: 55.5. $2000+

Z.11 Napkin rings. Original box, 2.0"h x 3.25"w x 2.75"d. Rings, 1.38"h x 2.0"w. Backstamp: 27.1. Set, $160-200.

Z.9 Place card holders. 1.75"h x 1.38"w. Backstamp: J.1. Each, $80-100.

Z.12 Shaving mug. 3.88"h x 3.88"w. Backstamp: 27.1. $130-160.

Z.15 Double spooner. 2.25"h x 6.30"w x 3.63"d. Backstamp: 27.0. $70-100.

Z.13 Double spooner. 2.25"h x 6.30"w x 3.63"d. Backstamp: 27.0. $70-100.

Z.14 Double spooner. 2.25"h x 6.30"w x 3.63"d. Backstamp: 27.1. $90-130.

Z.16 Spooner. 2.5"h x 7.88"w x 1.75"d. Backstamp: 27.1. $50-70.

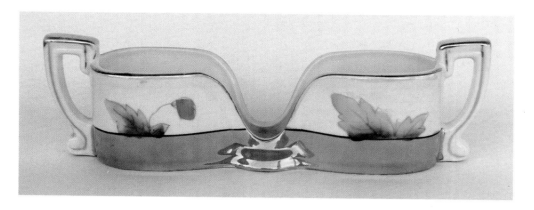

Z.16A Reverse of Z.16.

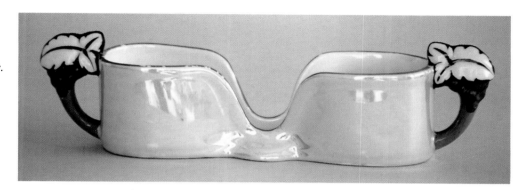

Z.17 Spooner. 2.25"h x 8.25"w.
Backstamp: 27.1. $50-70.

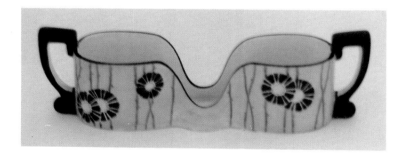

Z.18 Spooner. 2.38"h x 8.0"w. Backstamp: 27.0. $50-70.

Z.20 Toast rack. 3.5"h x 5.5"w x 3.38"d.
Backstamp: 27.0. $90-120.

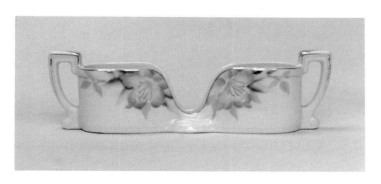

Z.19 Spooner. Azalea Larkin #189. 2.0"h x 8.13"w. Backstamp: 29.1
(19322). $80-100.

Z.21 Toast rack. 2.25"h x 5.5"w. Backstamp: 27.1. $50-80.

Z.24 Toothpick holders. 2.25"h x 1.63"w. Backstamp: 27.0. Each, $20-30.

Z.22 Toast rack. 2.25"h x 5.5"w. Backstamp: 27.1. $40-60.

Z.25 Toothpick holder. 2.0"h x 2.75"w. Backstamp: 27.1. $40-50.

Z.23 Toothpick holder. 2.13"h x 1.63"w. Backstamp: 27.0. $70-90.

Index